CREATE

AT HOME WITH OLD & NEW

ALI HEATH

MITCHELL BEAZLEY

CONTENTS

INTRODUCTION

Creating a home is one of the most personal expressions you can make, and deciding how and where you live – no matter how large or small the property – is a gift that brings with it the freedom to make choices, explore new ideas and develop your own curiosity, in order to express yourself in a way that feels right for you.

Home fulfils our basic need for shelter, but it is also the place where we hope to feel safe, loved, relaxed and inspired – connected to the people and things that mean the most to us. The spaces we live in can be transitory out of choice or fate, or if we are lucky, they can stay with us forever. When created with love and care, they feel special to wake up to and gorgeous to return to; they are connected to who we are and what we stand for. The one place where we feel rooted to the stories of the past and our dreams for the future.

In our modern world, the pressure of perfectionism has become amplified, often to the detriment of our peace of mind at home. However, more recently, it feels as if there has been a shift in behaviour and beliefs – the perfection so eagerly strived for is increasingly being swapped for lives and homes that are breaking free of design conventions and trends, in favour of creating spaces that feel personal, happy, responsible, and true to the lifestyle and values of their owners.

The joy once driven by having the latest, or bigger and better, is changing to spaces and objects that appeal to our senses, inspire our emotions, and inform our connection with the environment around us. Less homogenous and more visceral – when you choose to live the way you want, surrounded by things that make you happy, it feels more freeing, exciting, and timeless.

CREATE is intended to nudge us all to think a little more deeply about how we live in, feel about and decorate our homes. It is full of ideas for you to dip into and draw from, but they are intended as suggestions rather than a rule book, to encourage you on your own creative journey. This book is about living the life you imagine, nurturing your style and recognizing that it is okay to be you.

The book is split into three chapters: Chapter 1 *Establishing Your Style* encourages you to trust in your own creativity and consider a framework for your life, and gives advice on how to get started. Chapter 2 *Developing Your Eye* offers ideas on defining your palette; thinking sustainably; changing the way you shop; mixing antique, vintage and new; building collections; celebrating the handcrafted; lighting things up; layering pattern, fabrics and texture; choosing affordable art; and styling the details. Chapter 3 *Inspiring Your Journey* features ten inspirational designers, antique dealers, shopkeepers and a retired builder whose individual creative paths have inspired and nurtured their own unique mix of old and new at home.

It has been a pleasure to spend time with all the British creatives in this book and to connect internationally with designers that I greatly admire in Mallorca, Australia and Paris. I have loved our conversations and the chance to learn more about each of their compelling journeys. They all took a leap of faith to come on board with this book and many have waited patiently from our first conversations to reveal in full their new homes or remodelled spaces, for which I am eternally grateful.

Thank you for sharing this book with me – I hope that its pages encourage you to let go of perfection, to live the life you imagine and to create freely in your own unique and special way.

Ali x

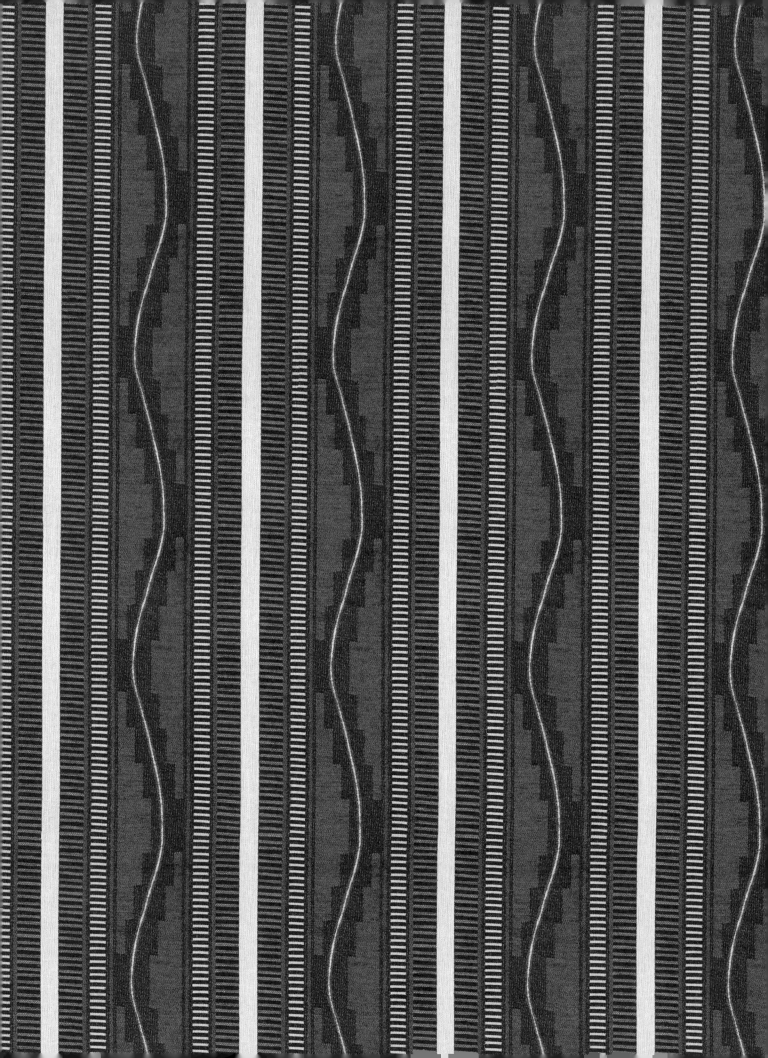

Establishing
Your Style

TRUST IN YOUR CREATIVITY

Trusting your intuition, taking risks and feeling out of your comfort zone are all part of the creative process. I hope by sharing the lessons I have learned, it may encourage you to let go of fear and create freely.

Before creativity there is always an element of chaos – but it is true that the best ideas are formed through a process of experimentation.

Creators are driven by what is and what can be – with heads full of ideas that have already taken shape, are in progress and still only exist in their imagination. It is never a race, so trust in the divine timing of things.

To create, try to reset traditional ways of thinking – by using fresh eyes you will challenge established patterns and the way you see things, and embrace the potential for new ideas.

Explore new areas and be imaginative – knowledge is based on current understanding, while imagination pushes new possibilities. At home this is how you create the magic.

Remind yourself regularly that you are creative – everyone is born with a creative side, but some choose not to believe this or suppress it through fear of failure. If you lose the monkey on your shoulder, you can simply enjoy the act of creativity and the pressure disappears.

You will learn valuable lessons by making mistakes – even if a design approach or effect doesn't work at first, you will learn from this and your brain will thrive when continually stimulated by new creative ideas. Success rarely takes place overnight.

Create what you thought was unimaginable – challenge, explore, question, care, seek, unearth, discover, collaborate, push, digest, manifest and do. There is no substitute for passion and hard work.

MIX IT UP For antique dealer
Lizzie Gordon @theoscarcollective
decorating is always about the find,
never the trend.

A FRAMEWORK FOR HOME

The idea of living well does not mean creating the perfect 'lifestyle' – everyday life is unpredictable, intermittent chaos is normal, and imperfection is good. **Home should be an expression of you and the future you dream of for your family,** a place where you can be yourself and connect meaningfully, with no pretence. **Creating a home is about intuition and taste.** If it doesn't come easily, be guided by suitability, individuality, proportion and simplicity. **To embrace antiques at home you don't need to be a connoisseur** – it is simply about the appreciation of form, materials, patina, and how pieces enhance the everyday. If you love it, then it is right. **New pieces will always have a place** but ethical and sustainable choices will help ensure a better future and more timeless decisions. **Freeing our homes from overindulgence is good for our wellbeing** and creates space for what we own to be fully appreciated. **Comfort is a necessity and touch affects our senses.** The choices you make about materials, furniture, and the tactility of finishing details will define how you react every day. **When budgets are limited, creativity has to raise its game** – switching your narrative from 'I want' to 'how can I' is empowering. **Elevate the ordinary to the unexpectedly brilliant** by creating something from nothing and avoiding convention. **Don't overthink it:** just go with what your feelings are telling you.

GETTING STARTED

Accept that not every house is perfect
There will always be the good, the bad and the ugly. Always a friend with a larger budget or bigger floorplan. Just remember, bigger does not mean better.

Don't look to experts for precise formulas
This is your home. Own your decisions, break the rules and make your space as personal to you as you wish.

Look at the shell of the house
Work with the bare bones you have, celebrate the quirks, decide what needs upgrading and introduce the best, ideally natural, materials you can afford.

Make light, air and comfort a priority
Think carefully about these features as they will always do much to enhance your home.

CURATED COLLECTIONS Sculptural studio pottery creates an elegant display on a staircase shelf in the home of Anthony and Karen Cull (see pages 62–79).

Seek inspiration everywhere
Fashion, art, architecture, films, books, travel, different cultures, Pinterest, Instagram and magazines are all great for generating ideas. A colour, pattern, shape, material, feeling or reaction might be the trigger.

Decide on your palette
It can help to look to your fashion wardrobe for inspiration. Often the colours you wear are the ones you can live with easily.

Work out what furniture is staying or going
Then make a list of the new items you need and the measurements of where they need to fit, so you are prepared when sourcing.

Find your red thread
This is simply something running through the design to connect the look: a colour, pattern, fabric or texture that will have a unifying effect. You can then layer complementary finds around this.

Begin a mood board
Use this to showcase your creative process and help filter your choices.

Layer your home as you would your wardrobe
If you just stick to the basics, your home will always be ordinary, but throw in a mix of antique, vintage, high street, designer and handmade, and a touch of the unpredictable, and you will elevate the look into something special.

Nothing good comes from following trends
You will never keep up and never create a home that feels true to you.

Luxury comes in many guises and for every budget
Whether it's a beautiful, 18th-century armoire, handpicked flowers or a well-placed thrift shop find, taking pleasure in the small things is a gift.

Keep it personal
Surround yourself with things that have an emotional attachment for you, and they will act as reminders of the different stages of your life.

Consider storage at the outset
This will be important if you are a collector to ensure still-life displays remain contained, not chaotic.

Practise and perfect
The layers create intrigue and are what makes a house unique and exciting. But if it feels too much, remove the layers, one by one, until the balance strikes a chord.

Books are one of life's great pleasures
Read them, learn from them, dust them, rearrange them, love them. Then close them and work out what your style is by practising on your own.

Never stop creating
If a room or your home feels complete, this will stifle your ability to be creative. The best interiors always continue to evolve.

Developing Your Eye

DEFINING YOUR PALETTE

Our relationship with colour is emotional – it affects our moods, senses and happiness, so colour choices are among the most important interior decisions you will make. Over the years, my home style has evolved from colourful to a mix of monochrome meets natural. Seeing so much colour in my work, I wanted our home to feel calm and restful, and this approach has helped keep my chameleon stylist tendencies under control. I hope what I've learned will help you too.

Only choose what you love – it should never be about trends or fashion, or a carbon copy of someone else's style.

Choose fewer colours – there are no rules for how many colours work best in a room, but in my opinion three to five shades are generally enough.

Use the 60:30:10 colour split – as do many interior designers as a guide to help achieve balance. This breaks down as 60 per cent dominant base (walls, statement furniture pieces, floor colour or oversized rugs); 30 per cent accent tones (bedding, curtains, blinds, occasional upholstery, small runners or rugs); and 10 per cent highlight pops (textiles, cushions, art and accessories).

Write down the feelings you wish to evoke – this will help make your choices clearer. Take inspiration too from the palette of a favourite object, a painting or the landscape around you.

Select any colours you want – perhaps all-white or monochrome, nature inspired or earthy, Wes Anderson bright or Bloomsbury Group rich, or a total move to the darker side. Once you have decided, though, use that palette consistently.

Consider how colours link throughout the house – avoid just looking at one room in isolation. You don't have to decorate all the spaces at once, but planning ahead will ensure the overall look feels cohesive.

Keep the base colour calm if you are cautious – then layer in more vibrant accents and highlights, as you become more comfortable.

Add more colour to change the energy – this is effective if you think a space relies too much on one colour or feels too bland or flat.

Incorporate a little black – this helps to anchor and add depth to any colour scheme. Try using a black frame, vase, stack of books or other object, or perhaps a piece of dark-painted furniture.

Don't be intimidated – just experiment and start creating. Your home will never feel dynamic if you only ever make safe choices. Always choose from the heart and be confident in the choices you make.

RED THREAD The dusky pink in each of these treasures at my home provides inspiration and connects the colour story.

BLACK & WHITE

Classic | Sophisticated | Iconic | Timeless

Having lived with this palette for a long time now, I know first-hand how restful and practical it can be. Far from feeling restrictive, a black-and-white palette allows antiques, pieces of art and inexpensive new or vintage finds to stand out, while also providing a backdrop that never dates.

For me, white is one of the most empowering shades to use in design: as a minimalist, all-encompassing foundation, as a base for accent colours, as part of a monochrome look, or as the start of a more neutral scheme. It brightens, calms and acts as the perfect canvas for textures and patterns. Alternatively, swap the emphasis from light to dark, and this will shift the atmosphere to moody and cocooning.

Simply decide which of the two hues is your lead and then punctuate your interior with the reverse to create contrast. Remember, you don't have to regard the colours as just two shades – there are a myriad of variations in between, from bright whites, chalky neutrals, pebble greys and smoky taupes, through to chocolate browns, warm charcoals and soft inky blacks. Varying the levels of saturation can also make the palette feel a little softer.

Layer highlight shades in natural tones, ochre, tobacco brown, green or rust, and these will add more depth and contrast. These shades can also be changed seasonally to enhance your scheme.

MONOCHROME CHIC In the home of Di Loone, touches of black are woven through textural bedding and appear in a vintage artwork and contemporary pendant light (see pages 80–93).

NATURAL & EARTHY
Simple | Still | Textural | Calming

Decorating with natural tones and staying close to nature's palette as a source of inspiration can bring a feeling of wellbeing to a space.

Nature can teach us much about simplicity, reverence and respect. Limiting colours and exercising restraint helps to create calm, restful spaces. Often, simply introducing some outdoor foliage or branches can bring immense textural appeal to your home and form the basis of a seasonal decorative look.

For Maria Le Mesurier, creative director of the UK-based furniture company WoodEdit, which she founded with her husband Paul, an inherent connection to nature sits at the heart of everything and informs all their life, home and business decisions.

The images opposite show how the spaces Maria creates for both herself and her clients are inspired by the beauty and authenticity of the natural world around her. Minimalist, whitewashed backdrops are offset by ever-changing sculptural branches and the clean-lined furniture designed by Maria and made by Paul. Sofas are covered in interchangeable, natural-coloured linens mixed with removable vintage fabrics – with five children, Maria balances a need for practicality and pared-back comfort with a unique, timeless elegance.

This style highlights the power of 'less is more' – earthy palettes aligned with a deep-rooted affinity with the natural world.

NATURAL FINDS Vintage wicker-wrapped wine bottles, Italian ceramics and antique linens complement the classic-meets-contemporary handmade furniture by WoodEdit. Lighting from IKEA and Baileys Home adds a modern edge.

BRIGHT & BOLD

Luxurious | Confident | Stimulating | Energizing

The use of brights and bolds can create a look that sits anywhere between the traditional, flamboyant, artistic, knocked-back, intoxicating, kitsch and full-on rock 'n' roll. How far you go with colour is up to you – it is simply about experimentation, and you can move up and down the scale of intensity as you wish. The use of strong colours can lift your mood, energize your home and inject both character and fun into a design.

Want to make an elegant statement? Then choose a maximum of two or three shades to give the colours space to shine. Keen to max up the zing? Then go overboard with your use of bright shades. Feeling overwhelmed and want to tone down the look? Then add plenty of neutrals and more negative space, to counter the dominant shades and introduce a sense of calm.

Colours positioned opposite each other on the colour wheel attract, while matching pairs will keep the scheme looking cohesive – think primary with primary, pastel with pastel. In my opinion, two similar dominant colours rarely work; variation is always good.

Introducing unusual colour riffs can help make your home feel immensely original. It is worth experimenting since the extraordinary combinations are often those that just gel unexpectedly, such as Lisa Mehydene's 'rhubarb and custard' painted kitchen, as she affectionately refers to it (see pages 162–165).

In the home of Russell Loughlan, shown opposite, primary reds and blues are painted in visually arresting blocks and stripes, to create a space that feels refreshingly contemporary.

ARTISTIC LICENCE The Farrow & Ball paints, Picture Gallery Red and Preference Red, add Georgian authenticity to Russell Loughlan's 18th-century cottage.

OLD MEETS NEW Super-talented HÁM Interiors artfully mix bold colours with unique antiques from Studio HÁM and individual contemporary finishes. Think glazed joinery walls, statement lighting, abstract art and bespoke, pattern-rich upholstery.

THINKING SUSTAINABLY

An eye for the old
Using layers of old furniture alongside newer pieces adds a patina and richness that are impossible to replicate. It also gives your space a sense of provenance and history that can be passed on to the next generation.

Recycle, reuse, repair
Learning to recycle and reuse what we have stops the constant flow of rubbish into landfill sites. We are discovering how to realign our throw-away culture, with repaired items increasingly regarded as art forms: think porcelain and ceramics brought back to life with the art of Kintsugi (a Japanese method for repairing broken ceramics) and fabrics patched, visibly mended or turned into decorative textiles by design companies like By Walid. This all ties in with our increased need to care about what we own: mending and fixing – not simply replacing.

Beauty in imperfection
The Japanese concept of Wabi-Sabi teaches us to appreciate the beauty of imperfection, meaning we celebrate, honour and embrace the patina and wear of time-worn materials. In modern homes, adding perfectly imperfect details such as antique fireplaces, reclaimed flooring, repurposed internal windows, vintage handles, patina-rich sinks and old taps becomes a way of incorporating that spirit.

Conscious sourcing
Using natural and sustainable materials like marble, stone, wood, limestone and brass, instead of homogenous and toxic alternatives, enables us to build timeless, authentic foundations for our homes. The same is true of textural layers made with centuries-old techniques: think linen bedding, hand-woven rush rugs, Zellige tiles, Tadelakt plaster walls and handcrafted willow fences. Buying locally, or from independent businesses who match our values, is increasingly important and satisfies our curiosity about a product's DNA and provenance.

Recycled and renewable fibres
Great comfort can be derived from surrounding ourselves with natural fibres that have been sourced or grown responsibly. Nature is restorative, balancing and healing, and many materials have the power to surprise us: wool is a natural insulator and 100 per cent recyclable; cork is lightweight and regenerative, with soundproofing and waterproofing qualities that make it wonderful for flooring and insulation; cob is virtually carbon free; and bamboo is of growing interest for its properties of strength and compression. Wood, hemp, willow and straw can all be grown regeneratively. Such factors are triggering designers to experiment and challenge conventional thinking and usage.

Regenerative design
With the climate crisis we are fast moving beyond reactive sustainability and 'do less harm' measures being enough. If sustainability is about reducing damage, regenerative design focuses on nurturing biodiversity, repairing the damage and removing carbon from the atmosphere, creating homes, city infrastructures and new timeless furniture in ways that allow the human and natural worlds to flourish side by side. The number of Passive homes – a concept referring to a type of construction that is truly energy efficient, comfortable, affordable and ecological – is likely to grow, and if the wisdom of indigenous communities, who have been designing regeneratively for centuries, gains traction, we could reconnect with important ancient ecological know-how and learn to co-evolve with nature once again, rather than against it.

PERFECTLY IMPERFECT The interior of the stone and timber cottage @sabi.stays, which is located in the Bay of Fires, in Tasmania, was transformed by Jessica and Fred Eggleston and showcases their appreciation of the Wabi-Sabi philosophy.

Buy less,
buy better.

CHANGING THE WAY WE SHOP

Our relationship with antiques has changed immeasurably – no longer seen as status symbols or for a privileged few, they have become more accessible and now appeal to people of all ages. With the notion of 'buying less, buying better' ever more prevalent, our choices are slowly becoming more discerning. Nowadays, less is more, quality wins over quantity, and aesthetic is favoured over perceived value. What was once an intimidating purchase has become an appreciation of craftsmanship, history and patina, and how that complements newer finds.

While antiques are enjoying a resurgence in popularity, our post-pandemic, high-street retail landscape has continued to decline. In the face of adversity, growing numbers of savvy antique dealers and interior designers have changed their fortunes by selling via e-commerce and social media channels. We have also seen the establishment of many dedicated online antique platforms, which are firing the imaginations of traditional buyers and new millennials. Antiques, once seen as stuffy, old-fashioned and elitist, have been rethought as aspirational, relevant and hot.

Although for me there is nothing better than the thrill of the find and being able to discover new pieces in the many beautiful shops, lifestyle stores and design emporiums that have reimagined themselves or recently emerged, antique shopping can now happen online in real time and from anywhere. This has made transactions fast, efficient and less open to bartering for fear of losing a purchase, which has allowed international audiences to shop globally and complete design projects from the comfort of home.

At the same time, the 'receive it tomorrow' delivery culture for newer pieces has triggered a growing desire for us buyers to source the more extraordinary, supporting independent makers in the process, and to feel more informed about a product's integrity. We are also enjoying a growth in the number of online curators, with companies presenting us with preselected e-commerce platforms that bring together thoughtful collections for us to peruse, without having to face the overwhelming trawl. The tastemakers behind the platforms bring a voice of trust and creative authority too (think Lucinda Chambers and Serena Hood, with Collagerie; Laura Jackson, with Glassette; Athena Calderone, with EyeSwoon; and Jeremiah Brent, with Atrio). What is also interesting about these curated sites is the mix of high-end with affordable pieces, as well as the placement of interiors alongside fashion and the everyday next to the aspirational.

The fast-paced speed at which the metaverse is becoming a reality, coupled with the introduction of augmented reality into many everyday purchases and interactions, will also continue to shift how we buy and use old and new finds for our homes. How the real and virtual worlds will coexist in the future is as yet unknown, but if the desire to create timelessly and with love and care remains at the core of antique and interior purchase decisions, a new and innovative way of sourcing, learning, consuming and living may emerge.

NATURAL EDGE In Alex Legendre's former home, collections and vintage fabrics are reimagined against earthy plaster walls.

MIXING ANTIQUE, VINTAGE & NEW

Choosing what antiques to buy is a matter of taste. Select finds that work alongside your existing new and vintage pieces because they complement your aesthetic, match your story and above all, because you love them. If you keep returning to the idea of suitability, longevity, proportion, form, patina and comfort, you will make decisions that feel right for you and your home.

THE HOUSE THAT THE GRAND TOUR BUILT

I have had a long-standing fascination with the idea of the Grand Tour, which was made popular during the 18th century when it was regarded as a rite of passage for many young, aristocratic English men. It marked the start of the UK's love affair with antiques, art and architecture from beyond its shores. Although a privilege granted only to the elite, it provided them with an opportunity for travel throughout Europe and beyond, to discover and educate themselves about some of the great creators, artists and sculptors of the ancient past and more recent Renaissance. At the end of a tour exquisite collections of cultural artefacts, antiques, art and curiosities would return with their new owners to decorate their homes and estates. The French Revolution in 1789 marked the end of these trips, but the legacy of the Grand Tour has lived on. If, like me, your parents took you as a child to visit endless stately homes, it may have influenced your creative eye and appreciation of the arts – something I am now very grateful for.

In the 1950s and '60s, American painter, sculptor and photographer Cy Twombly became revered for his collections of Greek and Roman artefacts and sculptures, which he masterfully curated alongside avant-garde art, both by himself and his contemporaries. Considered one of the greats among the interior design cognoscenti, Twombly's style mirrored *Gesamtkunstwerk* – a German term meaning a 'total work of art'. His creative process combined different art forms to produce a cohesive whole, and this vision remains inspirational today for venerated names in the world of design. More recently, James and Sophie Perkins reignited the idea of A Modern Grand Tour, following the Tour trail of the past and filling Aynhoe Park, their 17th-century Palladian house in Oxfordshire, with an inspirational collection of fine art, modern design and historical artefacts.

However, now that travel is increasingly accessible, the idea of a 'Tour' has become more egalitarian, with the duration of travel and ability to collect being dictated only by time, budget and a desire for enrichment.

Today, one of the collectors that stands out for me is the Danish designer, artist and tastemaker, Malene Birger. Her timeless collections of antiquities and art are united by a monochrome palette and are a personal high-low mix of items discovered during a lifetime of international travel – a true expression of her story, her creativity and her ability to curate objects and spaces with an intuitive, discerning eye. Beauty is seen in the ordinary and extraordinary, the inexpensive and expensive. Malene's finds were often sourced during her travels for new fashion collections, firstly as joint founder of Day Birger et Mikkelsen (1997–2002) and then as sole founder and creative director of By Malene Birger (2003–2014). Beyond fashion they have provided inspiration for her homeware collections and more recent venture into the creation of artwork, ceramics and jewellery.

Nomadic in spirit, Malene's travels have also inspired regular international moves, and the many homes that she has created in Copenhagen, London, Mallorca, Greece, Italy and now again in Mallorca all showcase her eye for sourcing. Antiquities, furniture, textiles and curiosities from Africa, Arabia, Asia and Europe have been reimagined among the more contemporary, while art collections, including lithographs by Picasso and Braque, are displayed alongside her own abstract works, sketches, prints, paintings and portraits.

Malene lives and breathes a visual language that artfully combines old and new: a signature style I love and one that is recognized and celebrated globally. I hope Malene's journey inspires you too.

SIGNATURE STYLE Malene Birger creates decorative hallways that make guests feel instantly welcome, inspired and at home.

INTERIOR ART This contemporary abstract face painted by Malene
is indicative of her fluid painting style.

OLD-WORLD TOUR MEETS
MODERN-DAY NOMAD

*Malene Birger | Danish Designer |
Artist | Serial Home Renovator*

Signature style? Monochrome, collected, maximalist, graphic, eclectic, functional. **Your desire to travel is driven by?** Curiosity and a craving for inspiration, new places, new cultures, flea markets, hotels and people – it develops my mindset. **What does travel mean to you?** For me, to travel is to live. My work is my life and my life is my work. Simple. I use travelling as a form of study and a source for new projects and ideas. **Do you embrace the idea of a Modern Grand Tour?** Well, in a way, as I have collected so much over the years, it feels as if I have curated a small, private museum. My passion for travel started when I was little. I 'travelled' to our neighbour, built a tent over their dining table, slept over and was always dreaming of when I could explore on my own. My first trip as a child, aged six, was to Mallorca, and my first trip without my parents was at 18 to Paris. A Grand Tour per year though, for sure. I have a Nile trip, a Botswana safari and a visit to Utah on my list for the next few years. **How has your nomadic spirit influenced your cultural appetite?** I have had the opportunity to buy some great pieces of art, furniture, decorative objects and textiles over the years, but I am always 'hungry' for more handcrafted objects, artisans, flea markets and charming hotels. **How has travel shaped the way you create your homes?** Hugely. My homes are nomadic in feel. Every piece has a story. It's a lot of work and a headache to ship things back, but I always manage somehow! **What have been your most memorable trips?** I started working in India 30 years ago, and I have some unforgettable memories from the early days when we travelled to unbelievable places in the mountains outside Bangalore. I adored my trips to Mexico – a great country and wonderful people, especially Yucatan. I also managed to see Beirut before the horrific attack in the 1980s. Petra, in Jordan, is probably the most outstanding sight I have seen – beautiful and extraordinary. **What has travel taught you about craftmanship?** Travel enables us to experience all the immensely special, traditional crafts that are practised around the globe – there is so much talent and creativity. Many of these skills are dying out. Younger generations are not as interested in learning, so time is our enemy. It's why I find flea markets so important; they have taught me so much history about how people travelled and took skills, pieces and memories from one place to another. **Favourite destinations to source things for your homes?** Spain, South America, Africa,

Mexico, India and Persia – if only I could go back in time. **Favourite finds?** Oh yes, there are lots, but I have too many to choose from – you know, I fall in love all the time. **Favourite markets?** Rome and Clignancourt, in Paris, at weekends; New York and Mallorca's Consell market on Sundays; and Nice on Mondays. I always source special furniture from Goldwood by Boris in Antwerp and strong 1960s and '70s furniture and lamps from other dealers there too. Auction houses in Germany are good for ceramics and eBay is very good for African art and inlay furniture. **Advice for collecting on a limited budget?** Invest in the best quality you can afford for your core main pieces; everything can be found in flea markets, at dealers or on eBay for really good prices. Buy some great accessories and add your personal style. Choose a colour theme and create a red thread throughout your home (see page 12). If you can't afford art, buy some cool posters and IKEA frames; there is so much available now. I sell some of my artworks as posters at The Poster Club, in Copenhagen. **What are you drawn to with your collections?** Anything that talks to me, but I'm especially attracted to Moorish, Arabian and African styles. I'm always hunting for original Italian designer lamps or furniture from the 1960s and '70s. I love the contrast and combination of decorative inlay furniture with modern clean designs – it goes so well with my monochrome and graphic art. **Current home?** A rural finca in Mallorca. **What does home mean to you?** A place where I can be myself, enjoy solitude, recharge my batteries or be with loved ones. A place to work, sleep, eat, entertain family and friends, and express my style and personality. It is also my business card, my showroom, my work, my art. **What is the most important thing for you when creating a home?** To create a warm and welcoming feeling, with an inspiring ambience and interesting look. And to renew my style and myself every time I move, without ever losing the core of who I am. **You leave a legacy with each home you create – is it hard to move on?** No, it's easy, it brings new opportunities, new energies…I have never thought about leaving a legacy behind me, though. **What informed your trademark monochrome palette?** The universe, night and day. I have always been drawn to black and white. The contrast. The trademark developed over time, as I became more confident in my interior design and as my collections grew stronger. Over the years, more dominant monochrome looks became integrated and it felt very natural and right for the brand. Suddenly, monochrome had become By Malene Birger's DNA. **You have a maximalist, eclectic style – how do you mix that with such a feeling of calm?** I think that the organization

CRAFT & CONTRAST Malene's rural finca, Alqueria Blanca, is a living-at-home studio and gallery for her collections of furniture, decorative finds and art. She created the sculptures using leftover marble and clay.

and proportions in my styling and spaces make everything feel calm. There is a lot of symmetry in how I style my home. I'm very proper. Mess is not for me. My first job was as a window dresser in ILLUM department store, in Copenhagen. I learned the skills of grouping and decorating and have drawn on the experience ever since. **Every room should have?** Grand decorative pairs of lamps, soft carpets and some Malene Birger art. **Every home should include?** A great kitchen space, where you spend most of your time; plus, practical rooms and lots of cupboards – you need them to be able to create a beautiful and stylish home. Who wants to look at a vacuum cleaner! **Do you think personality is key to making a home special?** I'm a storyteller and, yes indeed, I add my heart and personality. It's my life and work, so how can I not? **What triggered your passion for art?** What is life without art. Art makes you think and is always surprising. **You have inspired countless people with your design businesses – do you feel the worlds of fashion and interiors are closely interlinked?** Thank you so much! I see a link for sure. Interior design has become much more influenced by fashion over the last 10–12 years and the same in reverse. Both worlds are now better at working together, creating new expressions and possibilities. Fashion is fast and the interior and furniture businesses are slow. I think this is a great cocktail that meets in the middle. **Have you always painted?** I started painting in 2008, with ink on paper. Over the years, I transferred my artworks to canvas and linen, and I also do collages on paper or canvas. Living in many countries has constantly developed my style. **You have a very personal approach to framing – what comes first, the art or the frame?** My art walls are full of old flea-market frames mixed with new – the frame is nearly as important to me as the artwork, and I love to use simple, white IKEA shelves for display and so I can move frames around easily. **How do you nurture your own creativity?** I have always been driven. I'm my own gasoline! I wake up in the morning and start. I'm not waiting for influence or inspiration. Secondly, my life, my travels, my experiences, my brands, meeting interesting people and having great conversations. The more I work in my studio or in general, the better I get. **Do you feel the ability to create is within us all?** Yes! I found a great saying: 'Creativity is not something you are, it's something you do' by Tom Brinck…I find that so true. It says it all. **Who inspires you creatively?** The life I'm living and planning – since my plans always include new inspirations – and the great, brave, high-spirited people of the world. **What's next?** I'm renovating a charming, historical townhouse in Felanitx, on the southeast side of Mallorca, painting a lot, developing the ceramic side and planning my next Grand Tour.

EYE FOR DETAIL A brutalist 1960s cabinet, antique Carlo Bugatti chairs and 1970s Gae Aulenti Pileino table lamps are displayed with a Syrian headboard and Malene Birger art.

BUILDING YOUR COLLECTIONS

Personal collections are informed by our curiosity, our passions and our travels. They help tell our story, and knowing that they will survive us turns one lifetime into something that touches many others. The memories of where we found pieces, how much we paid, the thrill of the barter, and the provenance often shared with us by the seller all become as important over time as the finds themselves. If you are building your own collections, these thoughts may resonate.

Trust your own eye and not what is fashionable – if a collection sparks and excites your imagination, then it will remain timeless.

Nurture a sense of curiosity – when you seek the extraordinary in ordinary places, you will often discover things that no one else notices, and those unique finds can become the most treasured.

Collections are not necessarily collectables – they do not have to be of value and are often items that you cannot buy. At home, I am obsessed with my collections of seashells and pebbles, with every bowl being a reminder of my family and places visited.

Begin with just one or two items – I have been collecting antique coral, books, Astier de Villatte ceramics, handmade plates and old intaglios for many years. Each collection was beautiful when it was still small, but now, after many years, larger displays have taken on a magical appeal.

The thrill of discovery is addictive – spend time searching antique markets, secondhand shops, yard sales, auctions and brocantes. You never know what you will find.

Look to nature – this is a free and wonderfully rich source of inspiration for collectors.

Collect only what you love – collections offer a glimpse into your personality, so keep them true to you.

Consider your display – as your collections grow, layer them in cabinets, under domes and on coffee tables, tabletops and shelves. This will hone your creative eye, and tight displays will keep collections ordered.

Value hidden meanings – collections take on a new importance as you get older. They become part of your personal and family journey, and they can be passed on as cherished heirlooms.

AUTHENTIC FINDS The antique intaglios in the central image opposite are part of a larger collection of mine. Original mementos of the Grand Tour, they are increasingly rare finds.

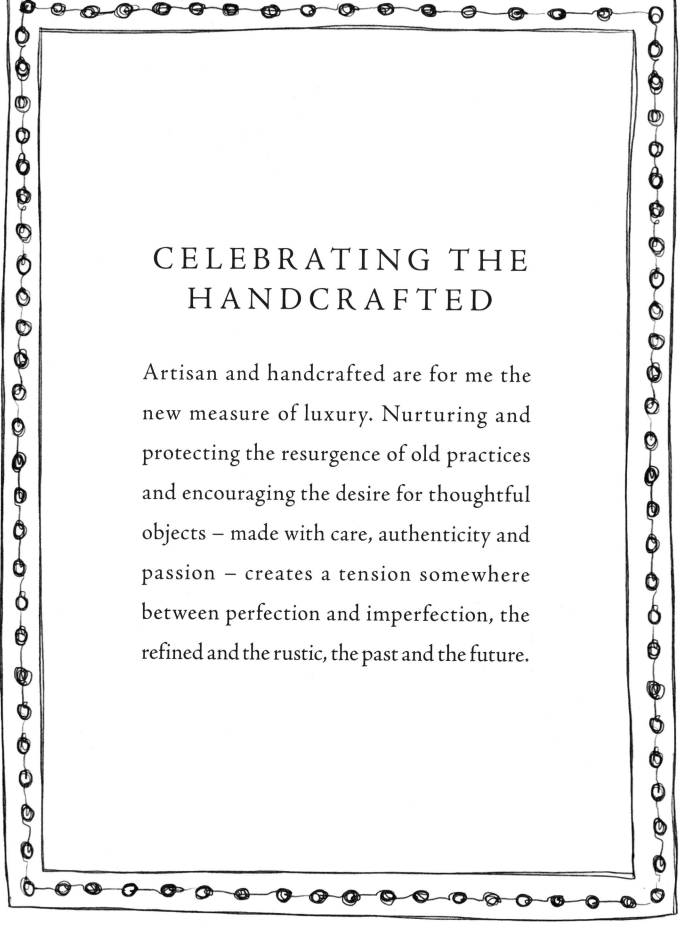

CELEBRATING THE HANDCRAFTED

Artisan and handcrafted are for me the new measure of luxury. Nurturing and protecting the resurgence of old practices and encouraging the desire for thoughtful objects – made with care, authenticity and passion – creates a tension somewhere between perfection and imperfection, the refined and the rustic, the past and the future.

Magic exists in the touch of the handmade.

LIGHTING THINGS UP

Lighting is a game changer in any room, although it is often overlooked. It is like adding jewellery to lift an outfit, but in a room it adds so much more than mere decorative appeal. Achieving the right level of illumination takes prodigious care and can transform the mood and feel of your home. Always ensure each light source you choose is also a beautiful piece that can be enjoyed by daylight too.

Consider lighting at the start of a project – establish early on how your lighting plan can bring together a mix of pendants, table lamps, floor lamps and wall lights. Overhead spotlights are purely functional – good to have as part of a scheme, but never THE scheme.

Hanging pendants and chandeliers add drama, impact and scale – and will make any space feel grand. In more bijoux rooms hang a chandelier low in a corner. Always hang lower than you think is necessary, as this will create intimacy and reduce overhead glare.

Vary the height, size and position of table lamps – display them on low stools and side tables or raise them higher on consoles and shelves. Battery-operated lamps can bring narrow mantelpieces to life and soften dark hallway corners with no electric sources.

Antique lamp bases make spaces feel unique – they can be picked up quite cheaply from eBay and Facebook Marketplace and at antique fairs and brocantes. In the UK, Ireland, Australia and New Zealand, lamp bases should come with a label stating that they are PAT tested (Portable Appliance Testing). If the base is not PAT tested, always get it rewired professionally before you plug it in.

Consider functionality coupled with design – a contemporary floor lamp positioned next to a vintage reupholstered sofa is practical for reading, but it will also add an old-new edge to the visual draw.

Always use more lamps than you think are needed – the trick is to illuminate a room softly to add ambience and a feeling of warmth throughout the whole space. In our kitchen I have ten light sources (overhead lights excluded). This creates a welcoming mood and encourages everyone to hang out and relax.

Handmade lampshades are more special – there are lots of companies that offer beautiful handmade shades in a wonderful mix of plain and patterned materials (see page 215). For me, these are preferable to buying off the peg. Within maximalist, more eclectic interiors, try mixing ikat, vintage sari fabrics, patterned weaves, jewel-like velvets and bold patterns. In monochrome or more natural schemes, mix old and new linen shades, with ticking, gingham, rattan, wicker, brass and metal alternatives. Breaking rooms up with variety is the key to creating schemes that catch and divert the eye.

Think of lighting as a decorative accessory – lights can be propped up, hung, strung across rooms and clipped to other objects. Move them around as you wish and change things according to the season to add more depth as the days get darker.

Never underestimate the power of atmosphere – always use dimmer switches and take time to enjoy the rituals of lighting a fire and burning a candle. They all add depth to the light, regardless of the season.

UNDERSTATED GLAMOUR
A treasured antique desk, foxed
mirror and ornate chandelier
add a sophisticated edge to
Alex Legendre's restful office,
in her old home.

MIX TO THE MAX

Layer lighting, both high and low, to enhance the atmosphere and creative appeal of a room. Try to combine shapes, styles and periods. More is always better, and when considered carefully, lighting choices can fulfil the need for both utility and beauty.

LAYERING PATTERN, FABRICS & TEXTURE

Dressing a room with pattern, fabrics and texture provides eye candy, edge and interest. These are often the layers that are left until the end of a project, but they are a vital part of what makes any room special. On their own they are undoubtedly lovely, but together they form a magical connection far greater than the sum of their individual parts.

Beauty lies in the mix – it is never about the match. To mix successfully, simply find your red thread (see page 12): a consistent connection that will create harmony and prevent rooms feeling chaotic and haphazard.

Vary finds from places, periods and makers – this makes it difficult to decipher what is expensive and what is not, which adds to the interest and appeal. The more patterns you layer, the more relaxing a room will appear, and this stops spaces feeling formulaic.

Choose a hero – whether a pattern, fabric or texture, this will help to anchor your main scheme and provide a directional layer for other items to bounce off. It might be a vintage linen for your sofa, a wallpaper pattern, a particular floor tile or a textural rug.

Opposites attract – mix plains and patterns, rough and smooth, sleek and embellished, luxurious and humble, tailored and worn, perfect and imperfect.

Mix only what you love – think stripes and checks, florals and plaids, leopard print and toile, ticking and abstracts, loose and tight weaves, bold motifs and understated patterns, hand-painted and block-printed, and always a mix of antique, vintage and new.

Introduce a neutral element – within patterned schemes this punctuates the space with a welcomed sense of calm.

It's all about the touch – the more pared back the palette, the more tactile and textural interest is needed. Think sheepskin, linen, hemp, wool, rush, cane, wood, stone, aged metals and rattan.

Make it personal – try a monogrammed blind with your initials, a favourite vintage fabric patched with care, handcrafted artisan baskets discovered on holiday or a bespoke wallpaper design.

Consider the foundations of your home as layers too – such as the patina of stripped-back old doors or raw plastered walls.

Contradictions add depth – think chequerboard floors dressed in colourful Indian rugs; an aged brass wall light, mounted on shiny gloss walls; or a sleek glass coffee table over a rustic sisal rug.

Incorporate the imperfect and quirky – this helps to elevate the style stakes and stops a home from feeling too formal or predictable.

AGED PERFECTION I collect bolts of antique fabrics and vintage grain sacks to upholster chairs and sofas, both at home and for private client projects. Mixing patterns and textures heightens the appeal of a space.

CHOOSING AFFORDABLE ART

Look to your existing collections and what you love
In the home of Alex Legendre (see pages 136–153), shown opposite, necklaces, bags, carved wooden shelves, decorative picture frames, old spoons, foxed glass panels and handwritten quotes are displayed creatively together, united by the palette and an affection for combining old and new.

Simplicity works
Consider focused collections of vintage plates, family photos or children's drawings washi-taped to the wall. Or hang simple tear sheets, postcards and sketches with a decorative clip.

Not all frames need to hold artwork
Sometimes it's about the charm of the empty surround.

Consider a themed wall
Display finds gathered on your travels, a cluster of artisanal bowls, hats or simple floral oil paintings or landscapes. Grouping similar items can help build up a collection quickly, as en masse they stand out and create impact, at minimal cost.

Anything goes
Fill your walls with inspirations, reminders, or nods to your personal ambitions, such as simple taped ideas for the house you long to build.

Nature is free
Blank walls filled with an arrangment of different dried grasses and flower cuttings simply taped across each stem can look amazing. Change the display seasonally and you will create a living wall that reflects the natural world around you.

Be curious
Make antique fairs, flea markets and yard sales your regular haunts for cost-effective gems. Regularly check out favourites on Instagram, Etsy, eBay and Facebook Marketplace or turn to curated online shopping sources that do the hard work for you, such as Partnership Editions, The Poster Club, The Saleroom, Art Gazette, Uprise Art and Artfinder. You can also visit fairs such as the Affordable Art Fair, Masterpiece and The Other Art Fair.

Visit graduate degree shows
This can be a brilliant way to buy affordable art and the pieces may well go up in value over the next few years.

Check out artist studios and galleries
Form relationships with them – this will help ensure you are one of the first to hear about new work.

CREATIVE WALLS An array of earthy finds displayed in the hallway of Alex Legendre's home (see pages 136–153) are reminders of different people and places.

THE ART OF DISPLAY

Building an art collection is a way of recognizing what connects your creative dots. However, displaying those pieces well can often feel intimidating. There are no hard-and-fast rules, but here are some ideas to experiment with.

Singular unframed pieces can be clipped, pinned and taped into place, either on their own or in collections.

When looking to display a set of connected artworks, unite the collection with a consistent frame and mount, then display in a grid format. Groupings of 4, 6, 9, 12 and 16 work well.

When hanging a statement piece of art behind a sofa, always position it lower than you think is necessary – just above and within the width of the back of the sofa.

Display small collections of mixed framed art together, whether contemporary, classic or naïve. Hang the artworks low down – just above a coffee table, or for a dramatic effect, from floor to ceiling. Never hang small artworks high up on their own.

Unite larger collections by colour or subject, then vary the mix of old and new frames. Keep uniform straight lines between artworks for a more formal look. Hang collectable with cheap, painted with typographic, vintage with abstract – this will heighten the impact.

To create a more haphazard gallery wall, consider a stepped approach. Anchor the collection with a central frame and step the outside frames up and down.

STYLING THE DETAILS

Styling is simply the art of arranging or curating an object, or group of objects, to bring to life the visual feel of your home. As a stylist, I tend to work intuitively: lots can be said about proportion, balance, harmony and unity, but the reality is there is nothing better than actual experimentation. These ideas might help you, but remember that one person's visual nirvana is another's nightmare, so trust your own eye, and if you love the look, that is all that matters.

Opt for maximalist or minimalist displays – these might be highly decorative or functional, colourful or based around a single shade.

Begin with one hero piece – perhaps a ceramic, painting, simple flower head or antique box, and let that piece inform the display.

Decide on symmetrical or asymmetrical displays – a pair of vases, candlesticks or matching decorative objects arranged either side of a painting or mirror will create a structured feel, whereas uneven displays have more fluidity and a quirkier visual appeal.

Mix heights, forms, textures and shapes – as this encourages your eye to explore. Books make wonderful display supports, so stack, prop, lean and layer them until the proximity and style feels right.

Variety is everything – combine antique with vintage, mix unique artisanal finds with a touch of high street, and always include the odd curiosity. The unpredictable brings excitement to a space.

Too much is never enough – a simple bowl of oversized lemons is an object of beauty, but abundance is key. You must have enough of such a detail for it to create impact. One lemon in a bowl won't cut it.

Add natural seasonal colour – branches and foliage are free and will have game-changing impact.

Use negative space – create opportunities for gaps, as this will produce a confident tension between objects.

Vignettes and details should never remain static – treat the process as a seasonal shake-up, an opportunity to begin again and rethink how things look and feel.

Have the courage of your convictions – if a display looks good, stop, but if you are fretting, take things off and start again.

Take your time – enjoy experimenting and over time styling will start to feel natural and instinctive.

HOME RITUALS Scented candles create atmosphere and make a home feel welcoming, while also enhancing visual displays. Favourite candles are sourced from Cire Trudon, Astier de Villatte, Merci, Fornasetti, Diptyque and Studio Oliver Gustav.

Inspiring Your
Journey

REIMAGINED THATCH

I first met antique dealers Anthony and Karen Cull, the creative owners behind the business Anton&K, back in 2015, when they had just completed the first phase of renovating their thatched cottage in the Cotswolds, in the UK. Over the years they have never stood still, and their first love of Swedish, French, Flemish and European antiques has been augmented by more contemporary lighting and the curation of unique artisanal pieces, which make up the collections they sell online.

Winding back a few years, their creative careers began very differently. Having sold their restaurant business in 2002, they moved to Mallorca, where Anthony and Karen took time out to rethink their focus. Renovating their Balearic millhouse, a passion for antiques, which had been quietly simmering in the UK, came to the fore, and along with Karen's interest in interior styling, a new direction was found. They returned to the UK in 2009, bought the cottage and turned their curatorial skills and creative eye into a new career – founding their now highly respected antiques business.

Never driven by trends, the couple set their own agenda and pace, and have not become slaves to ego or relentless personal promotion. Instead, they are curious by nature – simply sourcing what excites them visually and historically, while taking the time to build rewarding relationships with suppliers, makers, designers and homeowners all around the globe. 'We love the impact antiques can have on the energy of a room and a person; and it is the same for us at home. Pieces move around frequently, new finds supersede old, and the dynamic of our space is always changing to reflect our evolving taste,' says Karen.

Set in the heart of a quiet Cotswold village, the 17th-century cottage is surrounded by rolling countryside with views out to an ancient Saxon tower. 'We fell in love with the thick, wonky stone walls, the building's natural quirks and its inviting atmosphere,' remarks Karen. 'The cottage hadn't been touched for years, but the footprint meant we had space to add new, modern elevations that would respect and enhance the original integrity of the two-up-two-down structure,' she adds. From the front, the thatched cottage is quintessentially English, but from the back the traditional architecture now successfully fuses old and new.

The garden was excavated seven years ago to create space for a new open-plan kitchen and hallway which connect with the original cottage via a vaulted glass stairwell. This leads up to a new master bedroom suite and two more original bedrooms. Uncompromisingly simple and chic, the pitched ceiling spaces are capacious, lofty and uncluttered. They are curated with statement antiques, textural linens and contemporary ceramic

PERFECTLY BALANCED Primitive 18th-century folk art is enhanced with patina-rich antiques, modern ceramics and a repurposed Chinese jar turned lamp base.

pendant lights that add a refined and sophisticated modern vibe. More recently in the garden, a black larch-clad summerhouse has been designed and built from reclaimed materials – it is used as a quiet home office or outdoor retreat to enjoy the afternoon sunshine.

The interior of the cottage is decorated with the couple's signature light touch, pairing whitewashed walls with raw stone partitions and patina-rich, repurposed antique cheeseboard planks, which are used for the flooring and windowsills. In the sitting room, the vast inglenook fireplace has been transformed with a wood-burning stove, which heightens the feeling of comfort and escape.

The calming palette offsets furniture that is bold in shape and decorative in feel: handmade Belgian linen-covered sofas, striking antique chairs reupholstered in vintage linens, and a covetable collection of sought-after antiques. The space also features handmade decorative finds. There is always a touch of black in each room to add depth to the natural look, while patina-rich textures – think foxed mirrors, vintage rope chairs and stools, weathered wood tables, and oversized, smooth, ceramic pendant lights – add imaginative layers of interest and detail.

With antiques being part of Anthony and Karen's DNA, it is easy to see how much pleasure has been gained from sourcing for their home. Like their beloved Jack Russell, Molly, some things are keepers, including their Swedish mirrors and 18th-century secretaire filled with French ceramic medical jars. Also treasured are their hand-carved, Swedish dug-out bowls, the marble-topped kitchen patisserie counter, and the rustic dining room table that sits at the heart of many lively gatherings.

However, alongside this, there is also a more transient element, as seen in the 1950s Audoux Minet-style dining chairs, original dry-scraped sideboards, traditional Windsor chairs, decorated Chinese stoneware jars, rustic folk art finds, and mid-century modern antique ceramics, which give a nod to pieces that are fully enjoyed before they move on to new customers' homes.

Karen and Anthony have recently developed a love of art and their walls display an inspired mix of old and new: original antique oil paintings with 19th-century portraits; abstract 20th-century art, in the style of Terry Frost; mid-century modern art with iconic Spencer Fung prints; and primitive 18th-century folk art canvases. 'We like to find pieces that have a backstory and meaning – and when travelling we are always on the hunt for undiscovered artists in markets, in fairs and through less well-known dealers, tucked away down quiet side streets. These pieces add a time-worn appeal, sometimes with an occasional hint of colour – but always knocked back, to gently complement the natural tones throughout.'

Authentic and original, the look in this cottage is as much about the aesthetic as it is the atmosphere that their finds create, since for Anthony and Karen the lesson is simple: work and home cross over, and at the centre of everything a love of cooking, music and humour stops them taking themselves, or life, too seriously. Choices are based only on what draws their intuitive eye, what is comfortable and what is destined never to go out of fashion.

NATURAL WEAVES Vintage cheeseboard floors are combined with sisal flooring that leads up the staircase to the guest suite.

FIRED UP Vintage ceramics by Gunnar Nyland and a pair of Studio Viv Lee vases complement the contemporary feel of the Danish HETA wood-burning stove, which adds a modern edge to the thick stone fireplace.

CABINET OF CURIOSITIES An 18th-century Swedish armoire, home to a collection of 18th-century French medical jars and antique, handmade wooden plates, is offset against crisp white walls and modern shutters.

NATURAL BEAUTY A striking 19th-century French painting by an unknown artist adds feminine gravitas to the reading room. The dark canvas anchors a weathered collection of more masculine objects on the table in front.

BESPOKE MEETS ARTISAN Handmade cabinetry is intuitively mixed with covetable antiques, contemporary art and industrial lighting.

QUIET CORNERS Contemporary ceramics and natural-weave textiles from Toast add a modern edge to a rare 19th-century Gustavian Klismos chair, decorative Swedish mirror and elegant antique French chest of drawers.

ELEVATED STYLE Lofty proportions in the guest bedroom provide space for bespoke oversized wardrobes and handmade, conical-shaped ceramic lighting (from Anton&K). Decorative layers add quiet interest to the pared-back scheme.

DESIGN DETAILS The reclaimed stone
extension, with its glass walkway and
contemporary glazed doors, adds a
fresh edge to the original 17th-century
thatched cottage, complemented
by stylish architectural planting.

BEACH SHACK

Some homes speak to you – and for me, Drop Anchor is one of them. I have watched the Nancy Meyers 2003 film *Something's Gotta Give* enough times to know that my perfect beach house would have a whitewashed façade with a high-pitched roof and expansive glass doors to connect the interior with the breath-taking view. The interior would be airy and white with lots of battered wood and soft linens. I would walk early on the sandy beach, write in the window looking out to sea, relax in the outdoor bath under the dark inky sky, and chat with my family by the fire. This is the real-life version of the house I have imagined, photographed by my dear friend Marnie Hawson, and I am delighted to include it in my book. Maybe it's your dream house too? If it is, chances are, like me, you will probably also want to up sticks and move to Tasmania.

It is home to Di Loone and her husband, Anthony, who both fell for this gorgeous shack in Weymouth – a tiny hamlet in northern Tasmania – on a family fishing trip. Di grew up by the sea in Tasmania, and the couple had been searching for a coastal retreat that they could enjoy with their boys. 'The place has a quiet charm, unspoiled and restorative, with simple homes that have remained with the same families for generations,' says Di. 'There are no food shops or restaurants – we simply escape here with all our provisions packed, ready for slow-cooked breakfasts and relaxing outdoor suppers.'

After a six-month search and three failed house buys, Di found this original 1950s wooden shack with two bedrooms, a compact kitchen-living area, a small laundry and shower room. 'It was tired but had a wonderful, authentic feel. Our grown-up boys – Tom, 28, Will, 25, and Edward, 23 – all love to surf and fish, and it quickly became a place that we all wanted to meet up in, along with Tom's girlfriend, Annabel, who is part of the family too. After two years of getting to know the house, observing the light and making plans for the refurbishment, we decided to extend, not replace. The shack got under our skin, and we wanted to preserve it for the future.' The changes were designed personally by Di and Anthony, who worked closely with a local draughtsman and trusted builder, completing the project just before the Easter of 2021.

Three sets of new French doors were added to the north- and south-facing sides of the shack, framing a seamless sea vista as you arrive. 'The view and the roar of the Bass Strait hit you immediately – it feels hypnotic and instantly makes my shoulders drop,' says Di. The bedrooms and bathroom, which lead off the main living area, have been revamped, and a generous extension to the side and back perimeters has allowed room for a more capacious, vaulted kitchen-living-dining-room area and a third bedroom. 'We are remote, so must be resourceful with materials.

CALM WATERS An outdoor Victorian bath enhances the appeal of this enchanting coastal escape.

Much has been repurposed or reclaimed, such as Tasmanian oak boards, now painted white, and an old antique door, rehung with roller hinges to close off the living area from the new bedroom.'

The interior, which has been so thoughtfully curated, is indicative of Di's style. Keen to lead a more creative life, she swapped teaching for interior design, studying when the boys were little, before opening her interior store, Ecoco, in Launceston, Tasmania, in 2010, which sells vintage, new and handcrafted finds from around the world. Travel has influenced her style, and over the years buying trips to the UK, France, Belgium, Morocco and India have become regular sources for a relaxed mix of rustic furniture along with textiles and decorative objects, as well as select vintage and newer upholstered classics.

As Di explains: 'I always keep back special pieces for myself – mass-produced doesn't excite me, but the thrill of finding something unique makes creating a home compelling. Everything here is both functional and beautiful: plates and glasses created by local makers, Zellige bathroom tiles handmade in Morocco, and timeless one-offs, such as our vintage French butcher block turned kitchen island. Surfaces that show the marks of time and unite a sense of old with new appeal; and it has been an opportunity here to avoid the clutter of life, which can weigh you down, in our main family home.'

Within the open-plan area Di has cleverly zoned separate spaces, creating distinct areas for different activities, namely cooking, relaxing and eating. The wood-burning stove is a favourite spot – relaxing around the fire, the woody smell of smoke mingling with the salty air and favourite scented candles in thyme and olive. Surfaces are robust, not precious, and a mix of materials enhances the modern rustic vibe: hand-poured concrete worktops, a bespoke wooden kitchen, old brass taps, soft bed linens from bedouin SOCIETE, and a worn marble slab that sat at the back of Di's shop for years but is now transformed into a worktop around the laundry sink (usually filled with the catch of the day). Sisal and jute rugs help to delineate spaces, as does a mix of lighting, which includes enamel pendants, simple naked bulbs, cloth pendant globes and rope wall lights, sourced from interior stylist Sibella Court's store, The Society Inc.

Walls clad in original boarding are whitewashed in Popcorn by Porter's Paints and offset with kitchen carpentry in a dark Annie Sloan Chalk Paint®. Earthier greens and browns connect secondhand landscapes, nautical paintings, various textiles and abundant natural feathers, shells and botanicals – collected around the shack and on memorable beach walks.

Step outside onto the deck and you are within a few steps of the deserted sandy beach, which is alive with pelicans and kookaburras. 'Morning is my favourite time when the light streams in. The boys often go for a swim, while I practise my photography skills and enjoy that first burst of warmth on my skin. At night we relax on the new deck, surrounded by established indigenous planting, wild native grasses, tea trees and sheoaks, before settling by the fire. There is a magic here that is very hard to resist – it is our happy place and where we all reconnect.'

HEARTH & SOUL The cast-iron Nectre wood-burning stove lends a welcoming ambience to the modern rustic interior.

INSIDE OUT New French doors frame a seamless ocean view and bring a feeling of modernity to the original shack.

RUGGED & ROBUST Dark-painted kitchen cabinetry adds depth to the whitewashed space and is softened by weathered furniture, raw concrete work surfaces and abundant rustic textures. Natural beach finds add sculptural interest.

PRACTICAL MAGIC In a space
zoned into distinct areas for dining
and utility, tall white doors hide
functional laundry equipment.

PEACEFUL RETREAT Textural bed linens from bedouin SOCIETE, along with the cabinetry in the family bathroom, take their colour cues from the palette of locally sourced antique paintings and the outdoor landscape.

CREATIVE REPURPOSING An old door, original to the
beach shack, has been given a new lease of life and hung
from sliding roller hinges, which optimizes the space
between the bedroom and main living area.

MINIMALIST TOWNHOUSE

I got to know Anna Unwin at the start of her creative journey before she launched her successful online vintage store, AU. She is one of those people who are effortlessly authentic, just like the pieces she sells. A graduate of The Chelsea School of Art, in London, and a former interior stylist, Anna previously founded Maiden, a lifestyle and interior store in Primrose Hill, in the late 1980s. She then moved to her Georgian home in Cambridgeshire with her husband Willie and their three teenage girls, Olive, Flo and Boo, in 2010. From our first conversation I loved Anna's down-to-earth approach, and over the past six years she has remained true to her founding principles: selling only sustainable vintage finds, quietly challenging the mass-produced design norm that has been so prevalent in our industry, and championing the use of preloved furniture and vintage decorative textiles in new, cool ways – all before the word sustainability became a thing.

Anna has a refined hunter-gatherer's eye, loved by both private homeowners and leading names in the world of design. She curates interesting statement pieces, always vintage, but with an edginess that feels contemporary – think marble dining tables, travertine consoles, Danish antique chairs reupholstered in vintage sheepskin, and homeware created from time-worn fabric finds. Her online store embraces the ethos of connected slow design, where collections can be added to over time. At home these values align, and her private world feels calming and captivating in equal measure.

The lofty proportions of their Georgian home have recently undergone a major renovation, with Willie cleverly rethinking the vast 1,000-sq.-m (10,000-sq.-ft) former religious retreat and reimagining the space into a smaller family home, along with the creation of two separate houses that the family has now sold off. 'The space was just too big and despite grand ideas, the reality is we lived within set rooms and the constant upkeep meant other life choices had to be put on hold,' says Anna. 'We have now created a home that works for us as a family, where every space is used daily.'

Anna adds: 'I have loved the opportunity to rethink fundamental elements within our home. As a family of five, with two dogs, both Willie and I working from home, and a desire to live minimally and clutter free, storage is key; and we have created dedicated spaces that work hard – a walk-in boot room, a separate laundry and two office spaces. Living minimally slows the pace, but there must also be room for the reality of life to happen behind the scenes.'

The kitchen, a timeless Greg Cox design, fuses function with minimalist form. Sleek, floor-to-ceiling sliding cupboard doors cleverly conceal storage for cooking and kitchen appliances, while an oversized island reflects Anna's signature style: statement, never excess.

MONASTIC ELEGANCE Studio Ore brass tapware and oversized vintage bowls add statement impact to the minimal look.

Despite appearances, the ideas are often affordable – the immense dining room table is, in fact, made from two broken tables bases, topped with a piece of preloved travertine. 'At home, it's about trying to be clever with what we have, reusing and rethinking pieces to achieve a look, but without the price tag. Moving the kitchen to our former formal sitting room has changed the way we live – it's full of natural light and at the heart of the house, so we now feel connected to the garden, which is very uplifting,' says Anna. New Crittall doors lead to the terrace and are framed by 20-year-old sofas from Caravane. Cut into smaller daybeds, these are covered in layers of vintage mattress toppers and designed by Anna for the family and for Sid and Min, their wire-haired dachshund and old border terrier, to relax and hang out on.

Simple whitewashed walls form a relaxed backdrop for carefully chosen antiques, foxed mirrors, large-scale decorative finds, wall hangings and art. Painted in Linen Wash by Little Greene, the less obvious gloss finish encourages the light to bounce freely, while green accents inform the restrained palette – think collections of mottled sage onyx goblets and heavy marble bowls; moss-coloured plates; handcrafted mugs and tactile studio pottery; and rich khaki throws used as bed coverings and floor rugs. As finishing layers, sculptural branches and oversized indoor plants punctuate spaces with scale and drama.

Choices made ten years ago in the first round of renovations have stood the test of time: reclaimed herringbone wooden floors sourced by Anna from a former MI5 building and thick stone fireplaces from a dealer in France add gravitas to both the kitchen and dining room, endorsing Anna's motto of recycle, reduce, reuse. Statement lighting fuses contemporary rice paper shades from HAY, with a profusion of oversized AU antique stone and marble lights, alongside classic, fluted brass wall lights from Rose Uniacke. 'Home is where I feel grounded,' says Anna, and throughout the space the balancing energy of rare crystal clusters, quartz geodes and golden healers also adds an uplifting beauty and sense of vitality.

The home is an intentional mixture of contrasts: masculine with feminine; sharp lines with soft curves; rough against smooth; old repurposed into new. 'Every piece of textile in our home has been transformed from something else – an old bedcover into a headboard, former curtains into napkins, aged sheepskins into dining chair seat covers, vintage linen into cushions, dust sheets into roman blinds, old blankets sewn together as chic throws, and army mattress covers into cool sofa toppers,' says Anna. 'For me, the joy of buying vintage is about seeing things in a new light – like my fashion choices, I like to repurpose, sell on and buy secondhand – it keeps looks timeless, makes things more affordable, and becomes only ever about what you really love.'

Anna's home is very much a testimony to believing in the power of your own creativity. By sourcing only what inspires her and curating collections of reimagined, disparate vintage pieces, she has succeeded in creating a home and business that feel undeniably cohesive and original.

BEHIND CLOSED DOORS The cooking area is offset by repurposed vintage finds that are both decorative and functional.

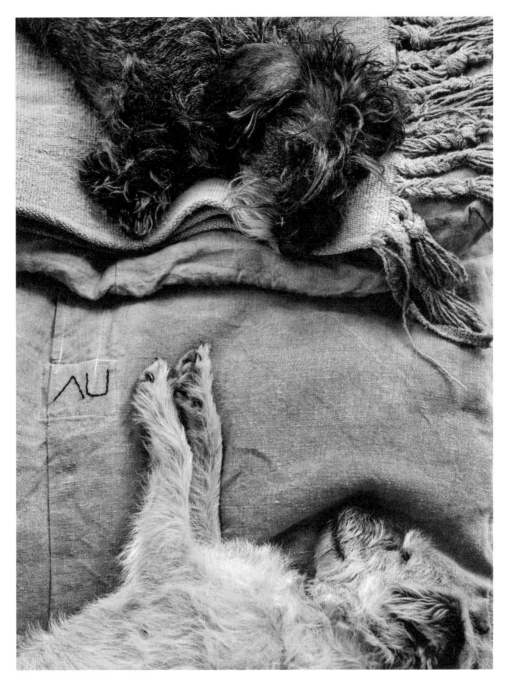

CALIBRATED COOL Vintage, new and artisan ceramics give the choice of covetable tableware a sophisticated edge.

LIGHT UP Steel-framed glass doors and a foxed antique French mirror encourage the flow of natural light from the kitchen and garden. The monochrome abstract canvas is by artist Oliver Hilton.

ANCIENT MODERN The ritual of burning sage sticks and infusing the home with scent is important to Anna, and the sacred volcanic stone incense burner from Katrina Phillips is a favourite.

STUDIO STYLE A vintage travertine table, an antique Danish chair re-covered in recycled sheepskin, and an oversized fibreglass floor light in Anna's home office are all indicative of her distinctive AU style.

WALL TO WALL In the laundry room, tailored cabinetry conceals the technological
workings of the house and provides abundant storage. Collections of chunky onyx garlands
and vintage wooden necklaces add decorative warmth to the children's bathroom.

BREATHING SPACE Less is more in the master en-suite. Simple mirrored cabinetry hides clutter while reflecting the beauty of decorative finds and modern Studio Ore brass tapware on pared-back travertine surfaces.

NATURAL EDGE The master bedroom is
layered in collections of earthy vintage linens
and hand-woven Turkish hemp rugs, from AU.
These are offset by shiny brass wall lights from
Rose Uniacke, a large rice paper shade from
HAY and an abundance of healing crystals.

RUSTIC BARN

The Harris family are firmly bound by tradition: for three generations they have been making the two-and-a-half-hour journey from the city of Melbourne to Merrijig, to make memories on this breathtaking piece of land that looks out across the Delatite Valley and Mount Buller – ski country in Australia's Victoria High Country. The love affair began when Terry Harris visited the area as a child. Then with his own young children – Wade, now 34, and Shannon, 33 – he rekindled that experience with riverside camping trips, before buying a 162-hectare (400-acre) property in 2007 and building a small, one-bedroom shack. Laid-back family get-togethers continued: at night hauled up in bunks, or in overflow outdoor tents as the family grew, and surrounded by kangaroos, all manner of bird life and vast star-filled skies. 'For us all, it was the perfect tonic, escaping the city and enjoying simple family days,' says Katherine, Terry's daughter-in-law.

Fast forward to today and the shack still remains, but sits gently under the wing of its impressive new counterpart, Coombs Hill, which is proudly positioned above on the ridge line. It is the manifestation of Terry's dream: to build a larger family house, rooted in the same rustic simplicity, but using a 160-year-old, repurposed Indiana barn as the foundation for the build.

'In his forties, Terry and his wife Cathy took a six-month sabbatical with their teenagers and travelled extensively throughout America. It opened their eyes to the beauty of the many barns that were being left to rot

and deteriorate, or simply knocked down for firewood; and Terry became determined to re-home one and bring it back to life in Australia,' explains Katherine.

In 2016, Terry found the perfect barn: it was carefully dismantled and each piece labelled like a jigsaw. Then two years later it was shipped to the site in Australia, where the planning was pre-approved, concrete foundations laid and glazing ready to be installed. This was the start of a two-year passion project: 'Terry even persuaded the seller, Kyle, who had never left Indiana, to fly to Australia and help him rebuild the structure – becoming firm friends in the process,' says Katherine.

Coombs Hill now cuts a spectacular dash on the dramatic landscape; and the monolithic, triple-height structure, with its symmetrical proportions and vaulted elevations, rises slowly as you approach via a simple dirt track. In the shadow of Mount Buller, the east-facing, external stone wall stands proud – a labour of love matched internally with a floor-to-ceiling fireplace. Each piece was laid by Terry over an 18-month period, using sandstone and mudstone collected by hand from surrounding paddocks.

Clad externally in dark grey Australian pine and with a corrugated tin roof, the barn now enjoys bespoke floor-to-beam, steel-framed windows,

HOME LOVE Coombs Hill was voted the 'Best Designed Stay' at the 2022 Airbnb Host Awards.

which can be opened on all sides to let the cooling breezes filter in. As you enter the 100-sq.-m (1,100-sq.-ft) Great Room through heavy steel doors, the scale of the room, which reaches a height of 12m (39ft), leaves you in awe, while the distinctive smell of the raw American poplar posts and beams grounds the space with a sense of provenance. These wooden elements contrast artfully with the contemporary polished concrete floors. Following the seamless connection between the barn and the landscape, the eye is immediately drawn across the oversized dining table – made to Katherine's design by Terry using leftover beams– through to the wooden deck beyond. Here, a second table crafted by Terry is a favourite spot for lazy breakfasts and long summer lunches, looking out across the plains.

Repurposing old into new, Terry (now a retired builder by trade) has expertly re-erected the structure, while bringing it into the 21st century with a hand-finished kitchen and five creatively arranged bedrooms and bathrooms that extend over three floors. Thinking sustainably, he has turned draughty and cold into cosy or cool on demand, with a 7-star energy rating, solar panels, reverse cycle heating, and an automated in-floor heating and air conditioning system.

The interior design was passed to Katherine (a former real estate consultant turned interior designer) and her husband, Wade (also a builder). They wanted to bring a sense of style and comfort to the home – to create a place for the family to kick back and relax. 'I wanted to bring together timeless pieces that felt elegant, comfortable and welcoming,' explains Katherine. Throughout, whitewashed walls offset the rustic structure and are balanced with classic furniture and edgier industrial cues. 'The Great Room is divided into different zones which enables us all to carve out time individually or together – my favourite time of day is always sat to the right of the fireplace, watching the sun rise over Mount Buller,' says Katherine. 'It's truly magical.'

Textural layers add the finishing touches and embellish the calm interior, as do the tactile furniture and natural accessories: think oversized linen- and leather-covered sofas, wool and jute rugs, soft linen bedding, heavy luxurious quilts, cosy throws and collections of handcrafted ceramics – Robert Gordon is a particular favourite of Katherine's. To add touches of more contemporary luxe, Katherine has incorporated elegant steel chairs, handcrafted ceramic tiles, stone baths and luxurious brassware into the evolving organic look, to create a feeling of understated luxury. The beams and steel window frames take the place of art, while earthy botanicals and sculptural branches found on the land create natural, simple displays.

'Time is religiously blocked out for us as a family, but we do now also rent the space for select groups and intimate wedding parties. It is a very special place and lovely that it can be shared,' says Katherine. Surrounded by nature, the house has had a positive effect on the whole family – and the spirit Terry so wanted to preserve is now also adored by his grandchildren, who love to listen to his stories while out riding with him on his tractor. With the barn and family so intertwined, it feels as if this legacy is one that is destined to transcend many generations to come.

MODERN RUSTIC The barn successfully accommodates a combination of extremes: old with new and dramatic with cosy.

KEEPING GROUNDED The surrounding landscape has gently informed all the decorative decisions at Coombs Hill, from the tiles, textiles and ceramics to the earthy botanicals found on the land and used to create simple natural displays.

RAW FINISH Corrugated iron and original beams create an industrial feel, offset by linens and old furniture. The vintage rolltop bath provides a relaxing retreat overlooking the Great Room.

REINVENTED COTTAGE

Since this beautiful cottage was photographed for the book, it has been sold, but it feels right to include the story of its former owner, Bee Osborn, as I feel she may inspire many others, safe in the knowledge that life's journey is not always straightforward and our creativity can be pushed as a result of adversity.

The path to finding a home is different for all of us – sometimes we move because we have outgrown our space; sometimes to move up the property ladder, or to downsize; and sometimes it happens as a result of unexpected change – becoming a place that the owner didn't expect to live in and then, having made it their own, never expected to leave. For Bee, this rural English cottage was exactly that, but in her case, letting it go and moving forward has been a lesson in the power of creating something special and believing you can do it again. Something she is no stranger to.

Bee's love of property began in her thirties when she suddenly found herself on her own with two children and no money. She had to switch from being a stay-at-home mother to one keeping the family afloat. With a passion for interiors, she took out a 100% mortgage, juggled a part-time job, and renovated and flipped the first of many houses, before she decided to back her passion for interiors and establish Osborn Interiors in 1998. Since then, Bee has built the business into an internationally recognized design studio, with a portfolio of residential and hotel work within the UK, St Barths, the South of France and Spain.

Five years ago, while living and working in London, Bee was looking to rent a bolthole in the country, near to where her third daughter was about to begin school. Having failed to find anything suitable, she discovered a cottage for sale in an overgrown plot on a chance drive back to London. 'The cottage, the former village post office, was rundown, but it reminded me of my childhood family home – safe, happy and nostalgically very familiar,' says Bee. So much so, it took just ten minutes for her to make an offer, three weeks to move in, and only six months to transition her design business to the area.

Often mistaken for the picture-perfect cottage used as a location in the 2006 film *The Holiday*, the structure was built in 1530 as a two-up-two-down. It has thick stone walls, an inglenook fireplace and a charming thatched roof, with a stone barn at the rear. 'The barn, added in 1700 as a stable for the post office delivery horses, was in a derelict state, but had enormous potential to connect to the main cottage,' explains Bee. Remodelling began at the beginning of the pandemic and took around six months to complete: 'My girls – Lara, 16, Tatiana, 30, and Hettie, 32, moved home, and we camped out in the original sitting room on mattresses, with a camping stove and no heating.'

AWARD WINNING Bee's cottage was a winner at the UK's prestigious BIID Interior Design Awards in 2022.

By altering the proportions and turning the crumbling barn into a connecting vaulted kitchen and dining room, Bee transformed bijoux and boxy into rambling and lofty – seamlessly bringing the 16th-century cottage into the present. Wanting to keep the integrity of the stables, Bee restored the original stone wall and clad the vaulted area with reclaimed schoolhouse timbers, which softens and cocoons the space. The old and rustic is contrasted with sleeker finishes, such as the clean-lined, handmade kitchen, an oversized artisan pendant, and new Crittall-style windows and doors that lead to the garden on both sides of the extension. 'I wanted the original and reclaimed to take centre stage and for more modern accents to enhance that rustic feel, but with a fresh modernity,' notes Bee.

Windows and sightlines in the cottage have been considered in great detail, connecting spaces and features, both internally and out to the garden. The pared-back rooms have been decorated throughout in a calming and restorative palette of chalky whites and soft green-greys – bespoke colours designed in collaboration with Fenwick & Tilbrook. 'For me, interior design is about investing wisely,' explains Bee. 'I like to mix high and low, and source carefully: my dream bath was found unexpectedly on eBay, which meant I had the budget to factor in a few more expensive pieces – such as the Porta Romana wall lights in the bathroom and the Pinch pendants over the kitchen island.'

CALM & CONSIDERED The capacious kitchen and dining space enjoys bespoke lighting by Hadeda and Pinch.

The relaxed interior decoration pivots around creating atmosphere, with lived-in textural layers of sisal, wool, velvet, linen and leather mixed with statement art walls: think personal collections of affordable hats, baskets and mirrors with abstract art that has caught Bee's eye. Hugo Guinness and Henrietta Carey are firm favourites, along with originals from many up-and-coming modern artists, sourced via Bee's daughter Hettie, who has recently started her own business, Art Untamed.

Clutter is kept to a minimum with well-thought-out spaces, such as the under-seat storage in the snug and dining area, the carefully planned laundry-meets-shower-room, and bespoke wardrobes built into awkward elevations. Even the boot room nook with its vintage cushion seat was designed around the antique basket – now used to store Wellington boots. As Bee explains: 'I can't function with mess – everything has a place and things are always bought to be practical, beautiful and comfortable.'

With the cottage enjoying a large following on social media, it was no surprise that Bee's calm and compelling style would attract the attention of many would-be buyers, and this interest coincided with a difficult time again for Bee in her private life. 'I never imagined I would come full circle personally and have to ever sell a home again, that I had created and funded on my own. However, letting go, it feels good to have restored the soul of the cottage, to pass this loved home on to the next family, and to take with me many design lessons that will help with the creation of my new home. Time here has provided me with the freedom to start a new personal chapter for my family, and that is to be celebrated.'

ARTFUL REDESIGN Bee has transformed the former kitchen into a family snug and designed the sofa to include valuable underseat storage. Abstract paintings and Hugo Guinness prints add a modern feel.

MIX & MATCH The original sitting room balances classic, textural furniture from Osborn Interiors with contemporary artwork from Art Untamed.

RECYCLED GLAMOUR The bateau bath was an eBay find and brings sophisticated elegance to the modern, but rustic, master bedroom en-suite. The cohesive wooden panelling adds an earthy warmth to the lofty proportions.

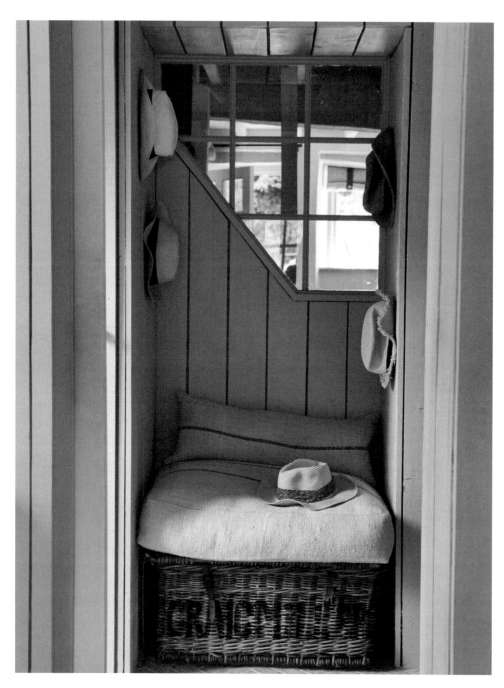

ALL IN THE DETAIL Bee used an old French basket, topped with bespoke grain sack cushions, as creative shoe and boot storage in the boot room nook. The wood-panelled laundry room, shown opposite, is also home to an additional shower room.

COASTAL SANCTUARY

An appreciation of antiques and the handcrafted sits at the core of who Alex Legendre is. She grew up in Brighton, on the UK's West Sussex coast, surrounded by characterful dealers, at a time when the city was at the epicentre of the antiques trade. Her stepdad was an infamous knocker boy, and from the age of 11 Alex bought and sold Art Deco silver marcasite jewellery and lace, while juggling under-age work in restaurants and cafés to support herself. Her childhood was tough, not pretty, and she had to learn independence out of necessity rather than choice. As an adult, Alex works hard because that is what she learned to do to survive. She also hoards stock because she knows what it feels like to come back from school to an empty home and a life that can change in the blink of an eye.

Alex's backstory does not define her, but it has shaped her drive, energy and creativity. She is gritty, yet down to earth; straight-talking, but empathetic; successful, but humble; motivated by trust and intolerant of disloyalty; and with a heart as big as her mad corkscrew hair and personality. At 15, Alex left home and school: finishing her art and art history exams remotely, she was awarded a graphic design internship, but without any financial means had to begin working. Four years later, with her now husband Keith, aka Ging, she began a new chapter in Asia and Australia, running restaurants and honing her creative eye for time-worn, sun-bleached furniture and decorative finds, before returning to England aged 23, pregnant with their daughter Mizzy.

The family lived in Hove for 18 years, and Alex co-founded the hugely successful general store, i gigi, which ran for two decades around the corner. Moving to Shoreham-by-Sea, West Sussex, in 2013, she transformed their small Edwardian house in her signature style (see pages 4, 29, 30 and 49, for example) and built a strong reputation for interior design and property renovation. An advocate of a life less ordinary (the title of her book published in 2013), Alex was seen as one of the original UK tastemakers for earthy, pared-back interiors. Inspired by her travels, i gigi sold antiques, handcrafted furniture, sofas and chairs covered in vintage linen, ceramics and clothing, and was a joyful mecca of one-offs.

So why am I sharing this? Because digging deeper in our interview for this book, it became clear the things that shaped Alex's formative years have also influenced her idea of home. This isn't simply about a perfectly styled house, filled with gorgeous things – it is about her imagining the emotional past of furniture, collections and curiosities, and the stories of previous lives well lived, to create a home for her family. One that feels soulful, happy and safe.

The move to this West Sussex home coincided with the decision to close the i gigi businesses. 'The market

NATURAL ON NATURAL Antique linen has been repurposed by Alex for bespoke covered sofas and lampshades.

was being flooded with mass-produced, high-street copies of what we had been sourcing authentically, and it felt the right time to change direction. I am half French, and we had always intended to live abroad in Italy, but with Brexit and the pandemic, our plans changed, and we discovered this place by chance.'

The building is a Georgian beauty, which was built in 1790. Acquiring their new home was a happy accident for the family, and within a year Alex had painstakingly restored the house, coach house and gardens. She also transformed a derelict greenhouse into an atmospheric and magical outdoor room, layered with well-chosen handmade textiles and featuring a welcoming wood-burning stove and stunning chandelier. The chandelier is Alex's version of art – one of many in the house, which throughout the space also reveals her appreciation for the humble and more utilitarian.

'The five-bedroom home had been owned by an architect and his creative family since 1963. Their paintings and ceramics filled the rooms and there was a very magical atmosphere here,' explains Alex. The family appreciated Alex's intention not to modernize the house, but instead to take it back to its original bones. Raw stripped walls are paired throughout with soft plaster finishes, and in the magnificent bathroom, simple, hand-trowelled micro-cement walls are offset by a grand, carved, copper bath, discovered in Paris eight years ago and one of a set from a palace in India.

Spaces are curated with an intuitive eye: antique sofas, chairs and lamps covered in vintage linen to Alex's creative designs; curtains and blinds; headboards, bedcovers and cushions reinvented from antique textiles; weathered furniture layered with natural finds discovered on walks and trips; and newer dining chairs carefully calibrated for comfort. There are also select finer antiques, such as a black, 15th-century, Irish display cupboard in the hallway and a patina-rich, pink-hued Swedish armoire and clock in the snug, sourced by Alex from her dedicated dealer friends.

The kitchen, designed by Alex, combines the best of old and new and it highlights her ability to think differently: sourcing one-off, exquisitely battered finds, such as the vast concrete sink and gnarly antique counter, repurposed as a central kitchen island. These pieces celebrate the beauty of real life and the marks of time in contrast to off-the-peg shiny and new. Open displays of ceramics, glassware and bowls sit among a mix of antique lamps and classic deVOL pendants. The original Aga, converted to electric and re-enamelled in one earthy shade, has been a wise investment for Alex and Ging who both love to cook.

Cabinets of curiosity and decorative walls (see page 46, top right, and page 54) have a *Gesamtkunstwerk* appeal – timeless pieces united by colour, aesthetic and form. 'Memories of an experience, person or place, they are all things that are beautiful to me and sit well together. For me, home is about creating a feeling, not the perfect façade – an escape where I can be myself with family and friends,' says Alex. 'When we come home and close the gates, I feel a deep sense of gratitude. There is a special energy here: a fantasy long held that has now become a reality – something I never take for granted.'

OBJECTS OF AFFECTION Antique chandeliers and chunky candleholders add to the ambience created by the rustic decor.

TEXTURAL DETAIL Throughout Alex's home, earthy personal finds enhance the raw bones of the house. Antique Indian carvings have been rethought as stylish wall lights and statement dried foliage elevates the natural feel.

PLAY WITH SCALE An antique bar counter repurposed as a kitchen island adds depth and patina to the kitchen designed by Alex. Open shelf displays, united by a subdued palette, enhance the space.

HARDWARE RULES Pendant lights and brass tapware from deVOL
have a classic modern elegance that enhances weathered finds,
including the large antique stone sink. In the adjacent pantry,
storage cupboard essentials add further layers of interest.

IN THE PINK A treasured Mora clock and antique 18th-century, dry-scraped cupboard, still with the original paint, bring a gentle touch of warmer colour to the neutral palette. The cupboard cleverly conceals media equipment.

PATINA & POLISH The curvaceous bathtub, hand-trowelled natural plaster walls and walk-in shower, have a softness that is juxtaposed by the clean-lined vanity and linear shelf edges.

CHARMED OASIS
A sculptural myrtle tree frames the entrance to the outdoor glasshouse, which has been transformed into a magical entertaining space. The weathered table, repurposed vintage textiles and striking antique chandelier give the space a refined Moorish elegance.

MAXIMALIST FARMHOUSE

There are a few things that supercharge Lisa Mehydene's sense of happiness: family, travel, vintage sourcing and home. As a former Advertising Director working for top advertising agencies in London, Dubai and Singapore, Lisa made a name for herself bringing prestigious brands to life. But on returning to the UK in 2015 with her husband, Hil, and their twins, Milla and George (now 11), Lisa was keen to begin a new journey. Nurturing her passions, she launched edit58, an online homeware brand that creates and sources one-off artisan and vintage finds, blurring the creative lines blissfully between home and work.

Living in London, the couple were keen to find a cottage that they could decamp to, and the less well-known areas within the Cotswolds, just 90 minutes from the city, ticked all the boxes. 'We were looking for a quiet sense of community, with space for the children to run free, and for us to enjoy extended time with family and friends.'

With Lisa and Hil both over six foot tall, low-ceilinged cottages felt claustrophobic, and relentless listings of open-plan conversions failed to deliver on character. 'Discovering this unique barn, part of a secluded farm, we fell in love with the rambling, 18th-century stone structure, its higgledy-piggledy flow and unexpected lofty heights. Everything needed updating, which provided the chance for me to play, but the layout and structural bones were perfect,' says Lisa. 'Filled with low dappled sunlight and with

views out across a river and open countryside, we were immediately charmed.' Indeed, looking up at the three-storey barn, with a series of dovecotes built into the thick external walls, you might mistakenly think you had arrived in rural Provence.

Legendary in the surrounding area for its mystical ley lines, the farm was once the base for the Beshara Trust – a charity that promotes a spiritual orientation in life – for 30 years from the 1970s, before the buildings were converted to private dwellings. Throughout, Lisa has intuitively worked her own magic, using a fusion of colour, pattern and texture alongside a glorious mix of vintage, artisan and select high-street finds. The walls are layered in swoon-worthy art – think flea-market finds, folk art, landscapes, portraits and an oversized Wayne Pate abstract – like me, Lisa is a fan.

'My sartorial style is very similar to my interiors, but at home the main thread is always vintage: traditional with a twist, never too wild and always sentimental; layered, but organized; colourful, yet knocked back. I'm not looking for energy from my interiors at the barn, instead I want to dial down the noise, to create a feeling of tranquillity and calm,' says Lisa. 'Most of the pieces here are low-cost and chosen to work within our budget. Namely, a drinks table purchased for £35

SCALE UP Reclaimed doors have added dramatic appeal to the opening between the hallway and sitting room.

at Kempton antiques market, and in the sitting room, a wavy-back vintage sofa which they picked up on eBay for £300 and reupholstered in Folies Bergère by Howe, along with a robust linen and contemporary stripe. 'I like the combination of old and new in one complete item – it adds a fresh edge and always makes for a more interesting story,' says Lisa.

Select antiques have been saved for, or received as gifts, but for Lisa it is never about the value of the object in question, simply the feel. 'Using things we had already and buying secondhand has helped us to customize a personal style, while thinking more sustainably. Everything here reflects our journey and has touched us in some way: a sketch brought back from holiday; artisan prototypes for edit58; a vintage yellow and pink Indian kitchen wall unit, unearthed at our local farm shop; paintings by the twins; or antique rugs bought at a brocante.'

Downstairs, one of the living room walls has been opened up and newly framed with floor-to-ceiling doors that were salvaged in France. The characterful kitchen meanwhile has been transformed with terracotta tiles, an antique Belgian display sideboard – a must-have, 'will-fit-somewhere-someday' buy – and a weathered florist's bench which has been turned into a kitchen table. The contrast with the more utilitarian British Standards cabinetry, reconditioned Aga and modern hand-painted enamelware adds depth, 'Hil is a fabulous cook and I love to entertain, so the kitchen is always at the centre of many great

ARTISTIC APPEAL Bauwerk limewash walls offset a Wayne Pate abstract, Astier de Villatte ceramic and decorative folk-art finds.

occasions, and always feels decorative.' Upstairs three bedrooms, each of which has an en-suite, have been updated; and throughout vintage cheeseboard planks from France have been repurposed as wide, patina-rich floorboards.

Colour has had a transformative effect on the cottage: soft pink Bauwerk limewash in the sitting room and Farrow & Ball Dead Salmon walls combined artfully with Pollen by Atelier Ellis on the new kitchen cabinetry – the 'rhubarb and custard' effect, as Lisa affectionately refers to it. And in the master bedroom, Farrow & Ball's Light Blue – a timeless favourite of Lisa's – is paired with handmade patterned prints by Antoinette Poisson.

Cosy, vibrant and welcoming, the house feels as if it has always been this way, and lighting adds atmosphere and warmth throughout. The oversized hallway lantern, inherited from the previous owner, is combined with assorted collections of high-low finds: 19th-century gilt bow sconces, brass wall lights dressed in hand-striped candle shades by Frolic Lighting; and Polly Fern lampshades. These are mixed with contemporary Zara Home lamps and Lisa's edit58 Ludlow lamp bases, a collaboration with Kelmscott Studio, topped with Alice Palmer stripy fabric shades.

Textiles, both old and new, are imaginatively layered – runners repurposed into colourful stair coverings and bathmats; vintage floral rugs used creatively as off-cuts for headboards; ribbon-tied blinds, cushions and upholstered ottomans; and patched antique Kantha throws transformed into one-off bed coverings. In this rural slice of heaven, Lisa's passion for colour, pattern and texture is a reminder of a life well lived.

FLORAL LAYERS A rug from Moldova is complemented by a bespoke ottoman, scallop-edged vintage curtains and repurposed tablecloth blinds.

HEIRLOOM FINDS The aged Swedish painted cupboard in the corner of Lisa's sitting room adds a Bloomsbury Group-style charm, an effect enhanced by the hand-painted Polly Fern lampshade and vintage shield find.

OPPOSITES ATTRACT New utilitarian cabinets from British Standard blend effortlessly with a glazed antique sideboard sourced in Belgium. Checked cushions and a runner from edit58 heighten the colourful, decorative appeal.

COOKING UP A STORM A reconditioned electric Aga works for the family's busy lifestyle and is paired with copper pans from Mauviel. The plates are modern transferware styles from Zara Home.

WORK & PLAY The first-floor study-meets-playroom is home to a profusion of pattern and texture. The wallpaper is by Pierre Frey and the vintage armchair is covered with Claremont's Nathalie fabric, upholstered by John Haswell.

ROUGH WITH SMOOTH The green gloss bath panelling enhances details in the Wayne Pate tiles for Balineum. The bathmat, and the headboard and blinds in the bedroom opposite, are made from edit58 vintage rugs. The painting 'White Vase' above the bed is by Rosie Harbottle.

TOP FLOOR OASIS In the master bedroom, Antoinette Poisson framed prints complement a bespoke floral headboard and vintage Indian Kantha throw. Kelmscott Studio's Ludlow lamp base for edit58 is paired with an Alice Palmer shade, embroidered by Cressida Jamieson.

CITY BOLTHOLE

There are many things I love about Paris: the architecture, antique markets, galleries and energy; the historic shop of my favourite ceramicist, Astier de Villatte, on the rue Saint Honoré; the lifestyle store Merci and its enchanting library; the inner courtyard at Hôtel Costes; and precious memories of my children sailing vintage pond yachts in the Jardin des Tuileries. However, one of my favourite discoveries is the wonderful work of the Parisian-based interior designer Marianne Evennou, who for me is one of the most talented interior designers of our time.

As an interior designer, Marianne's style is always compelling and visionary. She finds joy not in the size of a project, but in the atmosphere of the space and how it feels and flows, the provenance of the visual story, and the way colour, light and materials interact. Her signature style is instantly recognizable, yet each project is highly unique. She remains amazingly humble, concerned only with imagining, dreaming and listening carefully to her clients, and producing intricate plans that inspire. She has no interest in worrying about external opinions or trends.

'I like to keep the integrity of a place – in Paris, it is quite often the mouldings, chimneys, wooden floors and tiles that carry a timeless story,' explains Marianne. Globalized interior decoration does not appeal; instead she looks into the soul of a building and her client's mind to 'create a personal, imaginary museum – a second skin that protects and helps you face the outside world. It has nothing to do with social image, but is more a quest to discover who we really are'.

Marianne grew up in both France and Holland; and her somewhat nomadic existence instilled a love of home and a desire for roots. She met her husband Franck, a celebrated sculptor, furniture designer and artist, when she was 18. Forty-five years later, they now live in a former 1950s factory, 45 minutes from Paris, having moved from a nearby 17th-century monastery. Marianne's career has evolved creatively, moving from economic researcher to founder of a limited-edition artisanal rug company and marketing her husband's work. Then, at 50, she changed direction and took up interior design. 'I had already renovated several homes for myself and my family, but when our boys left home to study, I needed to be busy, and friends asked me to help them too.' These homes, applauded by the press, raised Marianne's profile, and her self-effacing passion has become a quiet force within the design world.

Regarded as an exceptional 'colourist' – and a master of reimagining smaller spaces – Marianne has built a reputation for breathing new life into thoughtlessly carved-out smaller apartments, set within prominent architectural addresses, changing these spaces from drab bedsits to 'poetic urban huts'.

HARD WORKING Bespoke hallway storage keeps spaces clutter free, while rich blue walls add impact as you enter this city retreat.

This coincides with the decorative pendulum swinging away from the stress of owning and maintaining larger properties to enjoying elegant, more bijoux spaces that 'feel lighter, both financially and materially'.

In this city project, a 35-sq.-m (377-sq.-ft), fourth-floor apartment located in the chic 2nd arrondissement of Paris, next to the famous Place Vendôme, Marianne has transformed dark and open plan into compartmentalized and bright, with the living spaces cleverly zoned for cooking, relaxing, sleeping and showering. A dark-hued entrance hall transitions into the lighter interior, painted in fresh shades of cornflower, pale blue, soft pink and off-whites, with Marianne's trademark bands of colour adding depth and refinement to the sitting room walls. 'I wanted to heighten the circulation of light by creating indoor vistas that allow the eye to travel freely,' she explains. There's an oversized mirror in the kitchen and a new separate bedroom, framed by elegant, atelier-style windows that can link the room to, or cocoon it from, the main living area.

Marianne is an expert at creating contrast within a space. For example, she cleverly uses different flooring, textures and colours to distinguish and connect areas with their own identity. Storage is cleverly hidden, ensuring open shelves and tables are the domain only of the useful and beautiful.

'Even though I enjoy looking at a refined Le Corbusier home, I personally like to mix styles, materials and eras – the "total look" is not for me.'

KITCHEN ON REFLECTION A statement Chinese vintage mirror increases the sense of space within the open-plan layout.

Throughout, sustainable materials ensure a timeless feel: herringbone parquet in the living room and bedroom, chic marble in the bathroom, and Pierre Bleue slate floors by Ermes Aurelia and Granit du Zimbabwé worktops in the kitchen. As Marianne explains: 'I like to balance natural raw materials with unpretentious refinement; and simplicity with more decorative artisanal finds.' Think patterned wedding boxes from Antoinette Poisson, Lucia Mondadori vases, Atelier Vime lighting and candle vases, alongside layered textiles from Caravane, Pierre Frey, Textiles Français and Tensira. Art is always important: a favourite portrait from the gallery Maison Massol and an ink triptych above the sofa by Franck Evennou, inspired by a Puvis de Chavannes painting.

Lighting is considered functionally, decoratively and for its ability to create mood and ambience. 'I am drawn creatively to industrial lights from Wo & Wé and Zangra, wicker lamps and cones from Atelier Vime, and more modernist Biny Spot wall lamps from DCW Editions. I also love to draw my own lampshade designs. Atmosphere is for me much more important than furniture – it creates a sense of wellbeing, which is something you cannot buy. Simple everyday things like books, music, a scented candle, a drawing of your child, a photo that reminds you of a happy moment, a dog on your knees or a textural plaid are like breathing creative magic into your home.'

Indeed, with Marianne's unique ability to connect with buildings and people, in her work she successfully conjures an original sense of place and personality, combining old architectural bones with the new and handmade – so creating that elusively unique atmosphere which, like her, is a rare and joyous find.

DRESSED TO IMPRESS Modern lights from Merci, vases from Lucia Mondadori and a
painting by Frédéric Amblard add beauty and aesthetic appeal to the bespoke kitchen.
The blue palette delineates the space from the living area.

BESPOKE DETAILS A custom-made sofa covered with a pink Pierre Frey fabric sits below a triptych of bespoke artworks by Franck Evennou.

DEPTH & DIVISION In the small bathroom area to the right of the bed, Marianne balances perspective with discretion. Soft pink paintwork and fabrics heighten the feminine charm.

PRIVATE SCREENING The bedroom can be separated with curtains from the main living area or left open to optimize light. Modern textiles from Caravane reflect the palette of the vintage portrait from Maison Massol above the bed.

MANSION HOUSE APARTMENT

Chris Graves and Jolene Ellis juggle time. Our interview for this book begins in between meetings from their London hotel room and finishes on their train journey back home to Somerset. With a working life split between the UK and abroad – currently in Miami, New York, LA and France – they both thrive on being busy, having founded their interior design practice Clarence & Graves back in 2020, with Chris acting as the principal designer and Jolene as the studio director.

The couple met, 17 years ago, on the set of MTV, before forming their own production company and working as writers, executive producers and award-winning format creators. The duo's filmic, through-the-lens approach to design continues to inform their style – with spaces inspired by aesthetic image capture and storytelling. They strip back the view to get to the heart of the owners – a concept that filters into their own home, with a defiant rejection of stud walls and glass partitions (shower screens included), which, for Chris, ruin sightlines and how a space makes him feel.

The couple describe their former London home as Wes Anderson meets Provençal and their new rural Somerset apartment in a mansion house as an Indian-Georgian Revival. Such animated descriptions make it quite easy to imagine that the high-impact decor could verge on pastiche – but here the opposite is true. Their colourful home is neither on trend nor 'of the moment'. Instead, it is a beautiful work in progress and

very much a reflection of what they love, without the need for the contrived or theatrical.

The move out of London coincided with lockdown and a desire to embark on a new aesthetic adventure. 'We daydreamed about a *piano nobile* in Italy and the idea of lateral first-floor living. This was our wild card during the property search: moving from a four-storey city townhouse to a four-bedroom country duplex apartment – we were attracted by the height and light, the endearing quality of abandonment, the potential to transform it into an original revival, and the most unencumbered property views. We feel like custodians of a National Trust house and garden, with a surround sound of bulls, ewes and lambs,' says Chris.

With a colourful provenance, their apartment, set within a Georgian manor house, dates from the 18th century, with later additions made by Sir Edwin Lutyens in 1913, after part of the house was partially burned down by suffragettes. Then in the 1970s and '80s, the estate transitioned from a school when it was converted into private apartments. On entering you are greeted by high-impact chequerboard floors in soft blue and off-white – a fresh twist on the traditional monochrome – contrasted with deep terracotta walls and a bold House of Hackney floral wallpaper, offset

PATTERN MATCH Statement glazed doors connect a bold House of Hackney wallpaper used in both the study and entrance.

with simple Verdigris lanterns from Vaughan. The space then leads into the main living area through imposing floor-to-ceiling glazed doors, commissioned by Chris to supersize the connection between the rooms. 'You can stand in one corner of the apartment and see through every space, from the boot room into the kitchen, study, drawing room, dining room and library. It was a deliberate design choice, knocking through an original wall, and the impact on flow and light has been remarkable.'

By removing the 1980s mask, along with false ceilings, stud walls and windowless bathrooms, the integrity of the space has been reinstated, revealing the true grandeur and scale of the home, which is lined with 16 rural-facing windows. 'The conservation specialist summarized our renovation as having "significantly enhanced the heritage features of the listed building" – which was a proud moment for us.'

The interior aesthetic connects shared cultural and sensory experiences: rich colour palettes influenced by time spent in India and Morocco; noteworthy collections of books; and an obsession with fashion, leading to an 'accidental Gucci-esque kitchen palette' – with subconscious nods to dark green cabinetry paired with a bold, red-and-white-striped Ralph Lauren wallpaper (amusingly teabag throw-tested).

Art is also a passion and brings together a regard for old and new: antique oils and Georgian framed portraits among colourful abstracts, a favourite artwork from Blur's Graham Coxon and provocative

paintings from the likes of Henrietta Dubrey. There's also a small nude above the fireplace in the glorious upstairs bathroom – a favourite from a local Spanish artist in San Sebastián.

'We are inspired by the unexpected – a rural wreck of a garage with bright green Crittall or a can of lager brought back from New York by a friend who described the colours as "very Clarence & Graves". Inspiration comes from everywhere and is why we love to travel,' says Jolene.

Furniture is a mix of classic and contemporary: modern velvet sofas paired with a formal 19th-century mahogany gem covered in a bold green and cream stripe. There's a weathered campaign trestle table repurposed as a kitchen table, framed by simple cane chairs, and a well-worn dining table – their first purchase 16 years ago.

Alongside the affordable, a collection of elegant antiques has been slowly purchased as investment heirloom pieces that bear the hallmarks of quality and well-crafted build. These include Regency ebonized and gilt dining chairs, a beautiful, mid-19th-century burr walnut desk; an ebonized faux bamboo Howard & Sons table in the drawing room from Ralfes' Yard, a favourite local haunt; and a former shop counter switched up as a rustic kitchen island.

'We love the ritual of simple daily pleasures that change with the seasons: the early morning sunrise, the cool through breezes of summer and the lighting of the first fire in winter.' Their home is a projected embodiment of their real selves, and whether with family, friends or the myriad of waifs and strays that seem to congregate here at weekends, the space is as welcoming as it is brave and individual.

CENTRE STAGE An original Aga is matched with reclaimed LASSCO floorboards, vintage hearth tiles and modern deVOL lights.

SIMPLICITY & FORM The classic Hugo Guinness bird print and Song Dynasty pouring vessel (dated 960–1279 AD), displayed on the deep, green window ledge, are both from local gallery Wilson Stephens & Jones and complement elegant antique finds from Ralfes' Yard.

FIRESIDE In the dining area, the newly raised fire grate enhances the feeling of connectivity. In the master bedroom, vintage curtains were repurposed as a bed throw and a modern ceramic caddy by artist Claudia Rankin was sourced from local gallery Wilson Stephens & Jones.

BATHING BEAUTY Opposite the antique rolltop bath an open fire adds a feeling of luxury. The small nude painting is by a local artist from San Sebastián in Spain.

A FUTURE LEGACY

Matthew Cox's story seems an apt way to conclude the ten compelling creative journeys featured throughout this chapter. As a third-generation antique dealer, he comes with both an innate and learned understanding of periods, designs, materials and craft processes, which has earned him a unique place in the world of antiques. For Matthew, though, the thrill of the find is about not only the aesthetic of a piece, but also his inherent connection with something designed to serve a practical purpose. 'Knowing that a piece has been used by generation after generation for the same purpose we'll be using it, creates a continuous relationship that connects and comforts me, far more than if it marks a fleeting moment in time,' he says.

'As an antique dealer that's all I have ever been interested in,' says Matthew. 'It's never been about the buying, selling or collecting – for me, things simply need to be purposeful.' Indeed, for Matthew excellence in craft is initiated by need. 'We all need a roof over our head, a table to eat at and a cup to drink from. And through need furniture makers have refined the construction processes of everyday pieces, with tried-and-tested methods over many thousands of years. Today, so much commercially motivated modern design has abandoned the trusted ways of doing things, but for me there is great joy in turning over an antique to find it has been thoughtfully made by hand, with proven construction methods executed beautifully with skill and care.'

With the market for 17th-, 18th- and 19th-century antiques, or 'sleeping treasures' as Matthew likes to call them, becoming ever more depleted, he decided in 2017 to begin designing his own furniture and lighting – using his knowledge of antiques to create new made-to-measure designs, guided simply by the 'always out of the ordinary' ethos that has now come to define his company.

Working with his in-house studio team and long-term partner Camilla McLean, who is the creative communication and marketing brain behind the business, Matthew generates the ideas for their new sustainable collections, which speak to the craft and design sensibilities he so loves. All pieces are delivered with the legacy promise that they will be as 'essential and beautiful in 100 years' time as they are today'.

'My role has always been that of a curator or producer. I like to conceive ideas and take the form of a concept through to the reality of a final piece. It started with the restoration of antiques, but now, in producing new furniture and lighting, those processes have developed on a larger scale.' With a growing team of 16 people, their dedicated workshop in Stamford, Lincolnshire, in the UK, is a hub of creativity, with skill sets ranging from those of fast-learning young apprentices to trusted

SENSE & SENSIBILITY Collect only what you love, and everything will find its natural home.

established makers and skilled finishers, who are now imparting their knowledge to the next generation of talent that Matthew is keen to nurture.

Each item in Matthew's range has important considerations in common: purpose in the design; longevity of sustainably sourced materials and a refurbishment and sell-back service; a human touch at the core of every piece made by hand; old and new elements of design infused into the creation of each piece; versatility due to the ability to scale pieces to any size; approachability, so that every touchpoint of the business feels accessible to customers; and an all-embracing aesthetic, with subtle nods made to global motifs in many of the designs, such as the Grecian bench and pyramid table.

There is a gentle assimilation that happens with Matthew's process – what starts as a client request or the seed of a new idea is slowly transformed into something special and new, with each new member of the team adding value to the finished prototypes. Photographing the studio, based in Matthew and Camilla's beautiful Georgian townhouse in Stamford, and in their nearby workshop, the team's dedication to the business and to Matthew as their figurehead is very evident.

The workshop atmosphere is engaging and relaxed; everyone is empowered and responsible – they are more a tight-knit family than everyday working colleagues. It's no surprise that many of them contacted Matthew directly to enquire about roles, as they make up a team that is clearly on the same page and have all bought into the vision. 'My father believed in giving me free rein as a teenager to explore my own thing, before studying History of Art and Design and then coming into the business, prior to setting up as an antique dealer on my own. It's the same with our team: I want them to believe in themselves and have the freedom to follow a path that feels right for them. There are no assumptions, nothing is set, and people are taken on merit, regardless of their age, gender or path.'

With change comes risk and Matthew is investing heavily not just to produce great furniture, but to do so with purpose for the long term. Inspiration is sought from everywhere and is an integral part of his usual day: his library of photographs and ideas is as compulsive as it is inspirational. As a couple, Matthew and Camilla's work and life boundaries happily cross over with their shared drive to build the foundations of their ambitious 100-year plans.

'The drive is not monetary but comes from a place of wanting to think and act more sustainably and with a stronger community approach. The need for nature and design to live more closely in tandem has become more important to me. Our design decisions need to improve outcomes for the whole world. Thinking in isolation is no longer good enough,' explains Matthew. Indeed, conversations move on to discussions around future stewardship – the selling of design blueprints and the establishment of workshops around the world to be closer to the end customer – and potentially adapting their product designs to indigenous woods, local labour and affordable transport costs. So, ideas not limited to the time afforded to one UK-based team – all of which adds to the excitement of their long-term vision.

LESS IS MORE Sculptural, primitive and decorative objects work in harmony with the original Georgian architecture.

At home, spaces are works in progress, effortlessly welcoming, yet fluid and ephemeral – creating an elegant backdrop for select antiques that have made the cut. Think glazed cupboards in the kitchen, weathered tables and consoles, and an enormous 19th-century display cabinet housing magazines in the studio. The industrial 'poetique' letters (see pages 210–211) were a gift from Matthew to Camilla during her former advertising agency days, as a nod to her love of poetry. More subliminally, they reference Matthew's own favourite quote from the designer Dieter Rams: 'Limit everything to the essential, but do not remove the poetry.' Throughout, new MC prototypes and finished samples complement the look – with no place for the superfluous or unnecessary.

Matthew and Camilla's client-facing approach is authentic and open. They have a growing international audience and their new website design, as well as the introduction of augmented reality to their online sales presence, shows they wish to bring their products direct to customers' homes. I ask Matthew about his thoughts on the metaverse and, like me, his head is already whirring with the possibility of how Web 3.0 is going to change all our lives and the opportunities it could bring for enhanced customer experiences. No one knows what's ahead, but it is coming fast, and being part of the discussion is indicative of the couple's approach.

Ask Matthew what he feels about the idea of leaving a legacy for the world and his response is charmingly self-effacing. 'I need a purpose in life, and am lucky to have found a clear one, which has been enabled by Camilla and a great creative team around me. The business name "Matthew Cox" has become synonymous with the ethos of the business, but is no longer just about me – it is our team as a whole. To know that my purpose can be carried forward with them, and for future generations, feels very special.'

'I never expect people to listen to me and don't want to tell others how to think or how to shop. If our messages are ones that resonate, then that is a wonderful thing – not something I set out to do, but wonderful, nonetheless,' says Matthew. 'If in the future, the business is associated with trying to do the right thing, then that would make me very proud. Connections with purposeful pieces have always been at the heart of my work, and for others to sense that connection with our crafted pieces in a 100 or 1,000 years' time, I would feel that our legacy had been fulfilled.'

MAKE AN ENTRANCE Prototypes, finished designs and treasured antiques complement the balance of old and new.

CREATIVE LICENCE The house is very much at one with its surrounding local vernacular.
The simplicity of the pared-back spaces means that rooms are always changing,
as products and ideas continue to evolve.

TO THE TABLE

Do as you please,
Eat from our plates,
Pass the port starboard,
Tell stories into the midnight hours.

Take everything you need
But give what you take.
All's fair and square.

When we're all the head of the table.

As cherrywood returns after a fire,
A scattered party finds its place again.

Fully restored.

Just the same
(But never the same again.)

And so the heart
With effort, with light, with love
Lives another day, another year,
Perhaps one hundred more.

Camilla McLean
MMXXII

SOURCES I LOVE

ANTIQUE SHOPS

Alex MacArthur Interiors
alexmacarthur.co.uk

Appley Hoare Antiques
appleyhoare.com

Brownrigg
brownrigg-interiors.co.uk

Chloe Antiques
chloeantiques.com

Claire Langley Antiques
clairelangleyantiques.co.uk

Doe & Hope
doeandhope.com

Emma Leschallas Antiques
leschallas-antiques.co.uk

Galerie Half
galeriehalf.com

Gallery B·R
gallerybr.co.uk

Gilli Hanna Antiques
gillihanna-antiques.co.uk

Howe
howelondon.com

Jamb London
jamb.co.uk

Josephine Ryan Antiques
josephineryanantiques.co.uk

Maison Artefact
maisonartefact.com

Max Rollitt
maxrollitt.com

Nimmo & Spooner
nimmoandspooner.co.uk

No.1 Lewes
no1lewes.com

Pickett's House
pickettshouse.com

Puckhaber Decorative Antiques
puckhaberdecorativeantiques.com

Quindry
quindry.net

Ralfes' Yard
ralfesyard.com

Spencer Swaffer Antiques
spencerswaffer.co.uk

Station Mill
stationmill.com

Streett Marburg
streettmarburg.co.uk

The Country Brocante
thecountrybrocante.co.uk

The Invisible Collection
theinvisiblecollection.com

The Peanut Vendor
thepeanutvendor.co.uk

Twig Ltd
twigltd.com

ANTIQUES ONLINE

1stDibs
1stdibs.com

Anton&K
antonandk.co.uk

AU
annaunwin.com

Béton Brut
betonbrut.co.uk

Decorative Antiques UK
decorativeantiquesuk.com

Decorative Collective
decorativecollective.com

Family Founded
familyfounded.com.au

Georgia Lacey
georgialacey.co.uk

Goose Home and Garden
goosehomeandgarden.com

La Place Antiques
laplaceantiques.com

Larusi
larusi.com

Lorfords Antiques
lorfordsantiques.com

Matthew Cox
matthewcox.com

Millington and Hope
millingtonandhope.com

Pamono
pamono.co.uk

Retrouvius
retrouvius.com

Scout + Bird
scoutandbird.com

Societique
societique.co.uk

Studio HÁM
studioham.co.uk

Tat London
tat-london.co.uk

The Blanchard Collective
blanchardcollective.com

The Bruno Effect
thebrunoeffect.com

The Drill Hall Emporium
thedrillhall.com.au

The Kairos Collective
thekairoscollective.com

The Malthouse Collective
themalthousecollective.co.uk

The Oscar Collective
theoscarcollective.co.uk

The Saleroom
the-saleroom.com

Thymka
thymka.com

Vinterior
Vinterior.co

LIFESTYLE SHOPS

8 Holland Street
8hollandstreet.com

Antoinette Poisson
antoinettepoisson.com

A Vida Portuguesa
avidaportuguesa.com

Abigail Ahern
abigailahern.com

Alex Eagle
alexeagle.com

Baileys
baileyshome.com

Berdoulat
berdoulat.co.uk

Casa González & González
gonzalez-gonzalez.es

Casa Gusto
getthegusto.com

Clic New York
clic.com

Cowdray Living
cowdray.co.uk

Cutter Brooks
cutterbrooks.com

Daylesford Organic
daylesford.com

Ecoco
ecoco.com.au

edit58
edit58.com

Freight HHG
freightstore.co.uk

Galerie MamMuti
mammuti.com

Graanmarkt13
graanmarkt13.com

Haus
haus-interiors.co.uk

John Derian
johnderian.com

Katrina Phillips
katrinaphillipsltd.com

La Métairie de Montgeard
lametairiedemontgeard.fr

Liberty
libertylondon.com

Merci
merci-merci.com

Nām
namstore.co.uk

Nest Home & Café
nest-home.com

Pentreath & Hall
pentreath-hall.com

Petersham Nurseries
petershamnurseries.com

Plain Goods
plain-goods.com

RW Guild
rwguild.com

Spiro
spirostore.com.au

Studio Oliver Gustav
olivergustav.com

Summerill & Bishop
summerillandbishop.com

The Edition 94
theedition94.com

The Evandale Village Store
thevillage.store

The Hambledon
thehambledon.com

The Hub General Store
thehubgeneralstore.com.au

Trove
thetrove.co.uk

Wattle & Daub
wattleanddaubhome.co.uk

Wesley and Willis
wesleyandwillis.com.au

ONLINE SHOPPING PLATFORMS

A Modern Grand Tour
amoderngrandtour.com

Atrio
shopatrio.com

Collagerie
collagerie.com

EyeSwoon
eye-swoon.com

Glassette
glassette.com

Kara Rosenlund
kararosenlund.com

The Artisan Collab
theartisancollab.com

The Society Inc
thesocietyinc.com.au

The Shop Floor Project
theshopfloorproject.com

HANDMADE

Astier de Villatte
astierdevillatte.com

Cathy Penton
cathypentonatelier.com

Elvis Robertson
etsy.com/uk/shop/
elvisrobertson

Franck Evennou
franck-evennou.com

Geoffrey Preston
geoffreypreston.co.uk

Hannah Tounsend
hannahtounsend.co.uk

Nicola Gillis Ceramics
nicolagillisceramics.co.uk

Pachadesign
pachadesign.co.uk

Soane Britain
soane.co.uk

WoodEdit
woodedit.co.uk

LAMPSHADES

Alice Palmer & Co
alicepalmer.co

Alvaro Picardo
alvaropicardo.com

Bloomsbury Revisited
bloomsburyrevisited.co.uk

Fermoie
fermoie.com

Samarkand Design
samarkanddesign.com

Sarah Blomfield
sarahblomfield.com

FABRICS

By Walid
bywalid.co.uk

Kirsten Hecktermann
kirstenhecktermann.bigcartel.com

Pierre Frey
pierrefrey.com

The Cloth Shop
theclothshop.net

Tobias and the Angel
tobiasandtheangel.com

ART ONLINE

Among the Pines
amongthepines.gallery

Anna Smith
whoamama.co.uk

Atelier Bleu
atelierbleu.co.uk

Caroline Popham
carolinepopham.com

Collins & Green
collinsandgreenart.co.uk

Domenica Marland
domenicamarland.com

Francis Gallery
francisgallery.co

Kalpa Art Living
kalpa-art.it

Malene Birger
malenebirgersworld.com

Marnie Hawson
marniehawson.com.au

Rob Wyn Yates
robwynyates.com

Saskia Saunders
saskiasaunders.com

Sassy Hardwick
sassyhardwick.co.uk

Spencer Fung Art
spencerfungart.com

The Coastal Studio
thecoastalstudioshop.etsy.com

Wayne Pate
waynepate.com

WSJ Gallery
wsjgallery.com

ONE MORE THING
Iconic interiors movies to make you swoon

Call Me by Your Name
Set in Italy, this is maximalism at its best, with layers of antiques, collected curios, grand pianos, paintings and faded textiles – not to mention the best library and fireplaces.

Breakfast at Tiffany's
Less is more in Holly Golightly's apartment and the half rolltop-bath-meets-sofa has talked to me for many years.

Something's Gotta Give
My all-time favourite Nancy Meyers film – perfect for Hamptons beach house drooling.

It's Complicated
Another Nancy Meyers film with a kitchen of dreams!

A Good Year
The perfect crumbling French chateau… turn off the sound and be mesmerized.

Practical Magic
The set was designed by Robin Standefer and Stephen Alesch of RW Guild notoriety back in their film days – the kitchen, potting room, outdoor veranda and picket fences all make my heart beat faster. This is set design and styling at its absolute best.

The Talented Mr Ripley
Inspired holiday living on the Amalfi Coast – timeless interiors and Jude Law… who needs more?

An American in Paris
The ultimate for ideas on small-space living.

The Children Act
The best art walls in a film and a great abstract painting spot for fans of Rob Wyn Yates.

Under the Tuscan Sun
The rambling wreck of an Italian villa in this film will make you want to move abroad.

Eat Pray Love
Hidden Italian apartments, the exotic colours of India and a dreamy open-sided house in Bali – warning: this film may trigger a serious case of wanderlust.

The Royal Tenenbaums
Larger than life, this is Wes Anderson at his best: a brownstone, clashing colours, Zebra wallpaper, retro furniture, taxidermy, wide window seats – does it get any better!

Nocturnal Animals
Tom Ford gets the minimalist interiors spot-on in this concrete and glass mansion – heavily curated, dark and intensely moody, it is filled with decadent furniture and covetable artworks.

The Grand Budapest Hotel
Marble columns, crimson carpets, pink paintwork, ornate brass lighting, oversized antique bathtubs and a backdrop of snowy mountains – the dream ski stopover.

Midnight in Paris
Time travelling through houses and periods – Gertrude Stein's salon is a treat.

THANK YOU

Creating a book is a privilege, made even more enjoyable by the team around me, and for this book I have loved spending time with a group of special creatives who inspire me and who have believed in this journey. Capturing each of their stories, it became abundantly clear that they have all carved out their lives with passion, hard work and a desire to fulfil their ambitions. You have made the book for me, and I cannot thank you enough for generously giving me your time and opening your doors wide.

I am incredibly grateful to Alun Callender, Emma Lewis, Marnie Hawson, Michael Paul and Michael Sinclair who have taken such beautiful new images with me specifically for this book. You have all done me proud – thank you for all your hard work.

Huge thanks to Brigitta Wolfgang Bjørnvad and The Sisters Agency for allowing me to use the striking images of Malene Birger's Mallorcan home; Grégory Timsit for your wonderful images of Marianne Evennou's Paris project; and Alexander James, Brent Darby and Rachael Smith for a few favourite images enjoyably shot together.

A massive thank you to my wonderful illustrator, Georgia Knowles, who worked with me for three months during her gap year from university to create the beautiful illustrations featured in the book. As *CREATE* publishes, Georgia will be graduating from university, and I know that she will have a fabulous career ahead. You are the best and I can't wait to see what unfolds for you. And to Nikki Griffiths, thank you for all your help; as always it was fun and so very much appreciated.

Many thanks to my publisher, Alison Starling, for believing in me; and to my brilliant team including Juliette Norsworthy, Sarah Allen, Caroline West, Katherine Hockley, and the whole extended team at Octopus for working so hard to make this journey happen.

To my beautiful children, Grace and Archie, thank you for your love and encouragement – I couldn't be prouder to see you both carving out your own exciting paths. And to my brilliant husband, Ian, thank you for always being there for me, and for your fabulous cooking and good humour that have all been so appreciated while writing this book.

Finally, a huge thank you to my dear friends who have cheered me on and everyone who has so kindly bought a copy of *CREATE* – you will never know how much it means and how much I appreciate your support. X

ABOUT THE AUTHOR

Living and breathing all things home, Ali Heath is an interiors expert, best known for her multifaceted work as a writer, interior stylist, creative consultant, designer and author, bringing to life people, spaces and brands with creative storytelling, both visually and in words.

For the past 18 years, Ali's work has featured regularly in prestigious interior magazines, newspapers and bookazines, including *Country Living*, *Elle Decoration*, *Elle Decoration Country*, *Homes & Gardens*, *House & Garden*, *HTSI*, *Livingetc*, *Modern Rustic*, *Red*, the *Telegraph*, the *Observer* and *YOU Magazine*. Ali collaborates with many leading photographers and her work is syndicated internationally by the Living Inside agency in Milan. Her own home has been featured in *Homes & Gardens*, *Modern Rustic*, *YOU Magazine* and *Country Home*, US.

Prior to becoming a writer and stylist, Ali enjoyed various commercial positions for leading companies in retail, marketing and sales, before moving into a creative and strategic role as New Business Director for a top creative agency. In 2002, Ali left the agency world to set up her own antiques and interiors business.

Ali's first bestselling book, *CURATE*, was published by Mitchell Beazley in 2020, and Ali is Contributing Editor and Creative Consultant for the second book from The White Company, *The Art of Living with White* (Mitchell Beazley, September 2022).

For more details, visit: www.aliheath.co.uk and @aliheath_uk

Create freely I have always been curious and interested in people, and over the years I have been lucky to share the unique stories of many established and up-and-coming creatives, both through the lens and on paper. My move into styling, writing and design consultancy wasn't a conventional way into this industry, and I am certainly not formally trained, but, like most creative journeys, I ended up here out of passion and with the tenacity to do what makes me really tick.

My love of antiques and interiors started at university while visiting my best friend's parents in Chester. Self-taught and highly respected antique dealers, they had worked their way up from nothing. Their home and outbuildings were full of more beautiful things than you could imagine and my time there had a profound impact on me. Those early insights and their infectious attitude fostered a burning desire to follow a path less ordinary for myself.

If you are reconsidering your own creative journey, my advice is: to be brave and follow your heart; not to feel intimidated; to work hard and not give up; not to let imposter syndrome hold you back; and to believe wholeheartedly in your ability to create. The reality is, most of us are paddling madly under the water, while trying to bring our dreams to life.

CREATE is a peek into my creative world and I hope the pages become well-worn, battered around the edges, and filled with scribbled notes for you to keep returning to. But, above all, I hope they encourage you to create freely in your own unique way, and to love reimagining the home that surrounds you.

With love, Ali x

HOME CONTRIBUTORS

Ali Heath
Writer | Stylist | Design Consultant

aliheath.co.uk @aliheath_uk
Photography: Alun Callender
Styling: Ali Heath
Pages: 1, 9, 17, 18, 22, 43 (above left,
above right, centre, below right), 45, 46
(above left, above centre, below centre),
53 (above left, centre left, centre right,
below centre), 59 (above left, above
centre, centre, below left), 215, 217, 219

Anthony & Karen Cull
Antique Dealers

antonandk.co.uk
@antonandkantiques
Photography: Emma Lewis
Styling: Ali Heath
Pages: 2, 12-13, 43 (below centre),
59 (below centre, below right,
centre left), 62-79

Anna Unwin
Vintage Sourcing | Stylist

annaunwin.com @anna.unwin
Photography: Michael Sinclair
Styling: Ali Heath
Pages: 53 (above right, below left),
59 (centre right), 94–111

Malene Birger
Designer | Artist | Property Renovator

malenebirgersworld.com
@malenebirgers_world
Photography: Birgitta Wolfgang
Bjørnvad / The Sister Agency
Pages: 35, 36, 39, 40

Di Loone
Shopkeeper | Interior Designer

ecoco.com.au @ecoco.com.au
Photography: Marnie Hawson
Pages: 19, 80–93

Harris Family
Builders | Interior Designer

coombshillbarn.com.au @coombs.hill
Photography: Marnie Hawson
Styling: Belle Hemming
Pages: 112–123

Bee Osborn
Interior Designer | Shopkeeper

osborninteriors.com
@osborninteriors
Photography: Alun Callender
Styling: Ali Heath
Pages: 124–135

Lisa Mehydene
Online Shopkeeper

edit58.com @edit.58
Photography: Michael Paul
Styling: Ali Heath
Pages: 53 (centre), 59 (above right),
154–171

Clarence & Graves
Interior Designer

clarenceandgraves.com
@clarenceandgraves
Photography: Emma Lewis
Styling: Ali Heath
Pages: 186–201

Alex Legendre
Interior Architect | Entrepreneur

@alexlegendre.interiors
Photography: Michael Sinclair
Styling: Ali Heath
Pages: 4, 29, 30, 43 (above centre, centre
left, centre right), 46 (above right, centre
left), 49, 53 (below right), 54, 136–153

Marianne Evennou
Interior Designer

marianne-evennou.com
@marianne_evennou
Photography: Grégory Timsit
Styling: Marianne Evennou
Pages: 172–185

Matthew Cox & Camille McLean
Antique Dealer | Furniture Maker

matthewcox.com @matthewcoxetc
Photography: Alun Callender
Styling: Ali Heath
Pages: 202–213

INDEX

Page numbers in *italics* refer to illustrations

INDEX

First published in Great Britain in 2023, by Mitchell Beazley, an imprint of Octopus Publishing Group Ltd, Carmelite House, 50 Victoria Embankment, London EC4Y 0DZ www.octopusbooks.co.uk

An Hachette UK Company www.hachette.co.uk

Distributed in the US by Hachette Book Group, 1290 Avenue of the Americas, 4th and 5th Floors, New York, NY 10104

Distributed in Canada by Canadian Manda Group, 664 Annette St., Toronto, Ontario, Canada M6S 2C8

Text and illustrations copyright: © Ali Heath 2023 Photographs copyright: © Alexander James 2023, 24–25; © Alun Callender 2023, 1, 9, 17, 18, 22, 43 al, ar, c, br, 45, 46 al, ac, bc, 53 al, cl, cr, bc, 59, al, ac, c, bl, 124–135, 202–213 215, 219; © Brent Darby 2023, front and back cover, 3, 20, 43 bl, 53 ac; © Birgitta Wolfgang Bjørnvad 2023, 35, 36, 39, 40; © Emma Lewis 2023, 2, 10, 12–13, 43 bc, 59 bc, br, cl, 62–79, 186–201; © Grégory Timsit 2023, 172–185; © Marnie Hawson 2023, 19, 27, 46c, cr, bl, br, 80–93, 112–123; © Michael Paul 2023, 53c, 59 ar, 154–171; © Michael Sinclair 2023, 4, 29, 30, 43 ac, cl, cr, 46 ar, cl, 49, 53 ar, bl, br, 54, 59 cr, 94–111, 136–153; © Rachael Smith 2023, 23.

ISBN 978-1-78472-855-7

A CIP catalogue record for this book is available from the British Library.

Printed and bound in China

3 5 7 9 10 8 6 4 2

Interior Styling and Creative Direction: Ali Heath Illustrator: Georgia Knowles

Publisher: Alison Starling
Art Director: Juliette Norsworthy
Editor: Sarah Allen
Copy Editor: Caroline West
Senior Production Manager: Katherine Hockley

MIX
Paper | Supporting responsible forestry
FSC® C008047